HOPE ON THE HORIZON

The History of
Horizon International

BARRY L. CALLEN

HOPE ON THE HORIZON
The History of Horizon International

Copyright 2010
by Barry L. Callen
All rights reserved.
Printed in the United States of America.

Published by Horizon International
P. O. Box 180
Pendleton, Indiana 46064-0180
Phone: 866-778-7020
Web address: **www.horizoninternationalinc.com**
To secure additional copies of the book, contact Horizon directly.

TABLE OF CONTENTS

Acknowledgments

Published histories of organizations tend to be valuable in proportion to the amount of relevant information that was available to their authors. In the case of this book, there was virtually no limit to what was available to me as the researcher and author. I am deeply grateful for this important fact and trust that I have handled this information responsibly.

I have had another distinct advantage. I have been the corporate secretary of Horizon International since the very beginning of this ministry's organizational life. Therefore, all of the financial records, minutes of meetings of the board of directors, and reports, letters, and publications of various kinds have been close at hand.

Yet another advantage should be acknowledged, again with much gratitude. My wife, Jan, and I were privileged to spend time at most of Horizon's African ministry centers in 2007. Neither of us were the same after those weeks with the orphaned children, their caregivers, and those special people who administer this work of God "on the ground" in South Africa, Uganda, Zambia, and Zimbabwe. Especially since 2007, Jan has been an enthusiastic Horizon supporter, including acting as the gracious hostess for several meetings of the board of directors that have convened in our home.

Numerous people have been helpful. With the assistance of the Horizon staff in the home office in Pendleton, Indiana, I have had access to all files – hardcopy, electronic, and photographic. Robert Pearson, the president of Horizon, was fully supportive throughout the research and writing process, setting aside valuable time for several personal interviews and then, as I requested, reading critically the first and final drafts of all chapters. Supportive also were key home-office staff persons Samantha Frazier and Gayla Morgan – I'm sure they, along with Robert Pearson, are relieved that this research and writing process is over!

Numerous formal interviews were conducted and requested written documents received by me during the years 2008 and 2009. All people involved shared freely and enthusiastically about their individual histories with Horizon and their observations about the ministry. To name but a few, my sincere thanks goes to: Ida Bell, James Bell, Deborah

3

Bergstrom, Donald Bergstrom, Lloyd Bowen, Diane Carey, Michael Carey, Joyce Chapple, Nancy Clark, Winston Clark, Charles Clevenger, Kelly Clevenger, Christopher Dancy, Eric Dwiggins, Doug Ehrgott, Sandy Ehrgott, Cindy Faulkner, Todd Faulkner, William Ferguson, Samantha Frazier, Bill Freije, Joyce Hartman, Larry Hartman, Mary Beth Jackson, Jeffrey Jenness, Timothy Kumfer, Gayla Morgan, Robert Pearson, C. J. Plogger, Bonnie Powlison, Lisa Scaling, Grace Sharritt, Jo Walter, Morris Walter, and others, including over twenty African ministry partners of Horizon who completed interview guides for me at their African Team Retreat that convened in Lusaka, Zambia, in the fall of 2008. For these and many other names, see this book's Index.

The expertise and generosity of *4-Minute Media* lies behind the DVD found inside the back cover of this book. Email inquiries to various Horizon leaders in the African countries where Horizon serves brought to me information and perspective of importance. If in the book's text there appears a direct quotation otherwise undocumented, it comes from one of these many interviews or emails.

The services of Rick Dodane are largely responsible for the quality of the cover and interior layout. Rick and so many others shared their memories and gifts without reserve. Apart from having all this cooperation, an adequate history of Horizon International would have been impossible. With it, however, the richness of this amazing story has emerged and now is available to the world. Since Horizon International is primarily the work of God, I end my acknowledgments by saying simply, to God be the glory!

Barry L. Callen
June, 2010
U.S.A.

DEDICATION

Chadd Bain was an important member of the Horizon leadership family in South Africa. He lost his life suddenly in a tragic accident in December, 2009. Left behind were his wife and partner in ministry, Kate, their children, and an emerging orphan-care ministry already providing for thirteen Zulu children. Horizon International mourns this loss and gladly dedicates this book of its own history to Chadd's memory.

Chadd Bain 1975-2009

A deeply Christian man, Chadd Bain embodied the vision of Jesus Christ for the poor, the suffering, and especially the children. Horizon's ongoing prayer is: May God's comfort surround Kate, and may God's blessing provide continuing ways to sustain the wonderful ministry to which the Bains were dedicating their lives.

This book goes forth in faith that, even over this human horizon marked so deeply by grief, fresh hope will somehow arise!

Foreword

All ministries, including Horizon International, arise from some early vision and then grow over the years through stages of development. These stages come to involve the ministry's expanding self-understanding and its shifting priorities as fresh opportunities come, new circumstances are faced, valuable partners are found, additional staff members become necessary, networks of accountability increase, and income fluctuates up or down. Horizon's mission is all about desperate children and divine compassion. It is God's idea and ministry; it also is a human organization subject to all the demands that any not-for-profit Christian enterprise faces. These pages attempt to reveal the challenges, changes, priorities, personnel, partners, procedures, and divine guidance experienced by Horizon during its first decade of existence.

One central aspect of Horizon's life has been unchanged from the beginning. This ministry has been dedicated to serving orphaned children in the countries of southern and eastern Africa. It has sought to do so in ways that avoid Western domination of African cultures and ministry partners. Horizon has attempted to identify the most effective means of accomplishing its divine calling. The assumption always has been that ministry effectiveness necessarily involves finding gifted and Africa-based partners. Once found, Horizon has chosen to come alongside and empower them in the pursuit of common ministry goals. It has hoped to be a servant body, working from the grassroots up on troubled African soil, respecting African partners and cultures, remaining open to local wisdom – and, of course, to divine guidance.

Horizon's ministry, not surprisingly, reveals periods of experimentation and varieties of partnerships. Flexibility has been necessary in the midst of differing cultural settings, circumstances of shifting need, unexpected events – sometimes dramatic and dangerous, the availability and dependability of leadership, requirements of local law, and the constraints of prevailing politics. How best to implement the deepest of Horizon's ministry commitments always has been impacted by such factors. Wisdom often is acquired only over time and with actual experience. This process continues.

Several Christian ministries, already active in Africa when Horizon International first arrived, soon came to blend into the Horizon family in various ways. Learning to live within this blending has required patience, prayer, sensitive leadership, and growth of understanding. It also has brought wonderful relationships, great joy, and increased ministry potential. It is hard to imagine Horizon having been effective in its divine call if people in Africa like Jenny and Cassie Carstens, Lucia and Tatenda Gunguwo, Nelly and Andries van der Merwe, Betty and Silas Atugonza, Alick and Vidah Phiri, and so many others had not stepped forward as invaluable ministry partners.

These marvelous African partnerships, it should be said clearly, would not have been able to function as well as they have if it had not been for a great support base that has developed in North America. This base is now comprised of members of Horizon's board of directors, an outstanding president, gifted and dedicated office staff persons in the home offices, the generosity of scores of pastors, congregational mission teams, individuals, businesses, foundations across the North American continent, and, of course, those many sponsors of orphaned children in Africa.

Horizon has been and remains a work in progress. In dramatically changing times, in the face of desperate human need, in substantially different social settings, and with a range of people and organizations divinely drawn to Horizon's vision of ministry, one wonderful thing is clear and has been a constant. God has been faithful to call, guide, teach, and provide. These pages are intended to praise God's name and encourage his ongoing mission of love in today's world!

So, in what follows, the reader will be able to see great need, daring vision, significant sacrifice, constant hope, experimentation, faith, change, and growth. Through it all, one will come to understand Horizon International, a relatively young Christian ministry that, on the one hand, was birthed and has been carried forward by mere humans, gifted and dedicated as they have been. On the other hand, and more importantly, what one will see is God at work on behalf of the children who have been caught in the midst of one of the more tragic health and social crises in all of human history.

Although it could go without saying, something is worth making very clear. All written histories are only snapshots in time, selected pieces of a larger reality, mere samples of people and events. The hope is that the pieces and samples have been selected wisely so that the picture given in these pages is accurate and represents well the larger whole – the whole that, because of limitation of space, cannot all be told.

Histories also are written from some perspective. In this case, the view is largely from North America as its people and resources have been gathered and employed in ministry on African soil. African-based ministry partners sometimes had their own histories before Horizon came on the scene. Horizon honors these histories, even if their larger stories cannot all be told here.

What is told here is presented humbly, gratefully, almost in amazement of what God has done through Horizon International in only a decade of time. This story is told for the children who have been victimized by an awful disease, unspeakable poverty, even by their own governments that sometimes have put greed and power before the well-being of people. May its telling be another way of ministering to the great needs of "the least of these," all loved greatly by God.

This book was written in thanks to God for the ministry calling, gifting, and faithfulness of Horizon International. It also has been written as one way to say "Thank You!" to the thousands of people who have made this ministry possible. In part, your reward can be seen in the smiling and healthy faces of the children pictured here. Yes, it's all about the children!

Barry L. Callen
June, 2010
U.S.A.

Trinity with Robert Pearson.
View her story on the DVD
inside this book's back cover.

Chapter One

FACING IMPOSSIBLE ODDS

When the worst human disaster in modern times strikes, what can one man possibly do to help? Especially if this man is in significant transition himself, what hope can there be? An answer actually came. It involved a calling from God in the face of apparent impossibility. The virus rampaged, the people died by the millions, and a multitude of children were orphaned and desperate. Then it happened. A dream came from God to a man willing to be used for the sake of "the least of these." Something new and wonderful was about to come over the horizon! While one man was particularly prominent, it was really a "God thing!" The odds were impossible; but, with God, all things are possible. Something new had to happen; something new was about to happen!

Do you remember those famous opening words of the 1859 novel *A Tale of Two Cities* by Charles Dickens? With the historical backdrop of the French Revolution, the novel begins with this paradoxical sentence: "It was the best of times; it was the worst of times." So it was back then, and so it still was at the opening of the twenty-first century. For Robert W. Pearson, a Christian minister in significant transition and actively seeking God's will, the conflict of good and bad was a little like the story of Joseph told in the book of Genesis. As Romans 8:28 later made plain, God is active in this troubled world, even in the midst of all the negative, working on behalf of the good. That certainly is how it appeared to Pearson – by faith, that is. However, determining exactly what God was doing and how he should be involved had not yet been clarified.

JOINING JOSEPH

The people of the world were tense, hopeful, wondering. There was much optimism in the year 2000. The time could be looked at as a new beginning for humanity in a new century and millennium. Even so, the worst could hardly be denied, especially in southern Africa. The plague was called HIV/AIDS and its victims were being counted in the millions. Our story involves one major attempt to address this human disaster. It begins very modestly, with just one man – and he too was in the best and worst of times in his own professional life.

Robert W. Pearson

Robert W. Pearson received his bachelor of arts degree from Seattle Pacific University in 1976 and his masters of divinity degree from Anderson University School of Theology in 1985. The honorary doctor of divinity degree awarded to him by Hope International University in 1998 carries an appropriate symbol, that of the awarding school's name. Pearson is a man of hope, a man with a big heart, one that beats on behalf of the Christian mission in the world. He has been referred to as "a catalytic visionary and networker." Such a man was ideal for launching a new ministry organization in the most difficult circumstances imaginable.

The home church of Robert Pearson, the Church of God movement (Anderson, Indiana), had recognized his considerable leadership and administrative skills. In 1998 the church brought him from his ministry in California to Indiana as the first elected General Director of the new "Church of God Ministries." This fledgling organization was the joining of a series of previously semi-independent national ministry bodies of the church. The first General Director was given the difficult task of guiding the new organization through the stressful period of getting started. The intention was to build into one effective and efficient body the several older cooperative ministries of the Church of God in North America. It was quite a challenge, but Pearson brought many gifts to the task.

After only two years of service in this new national post, overseeing many demanding aspects of the church's big organizational transition, Pearson and this particular role of General Director parted ways. Vigorous leadership in a major time of transition easily becomes a lightning rod that gathers many concerns and agendas into one hot spot. This is especially true when long-established patterns of relationships and control must be abandoned, the money to fuel the full operation of the new set-up is less than needed, and the pain of belt-tightening brings understandable resistance.

The year 2000 would be a fresh time for both the departing General Director and the struggling national church offices. Church of God Ministries, still finding its way, at least had been successfully launched and Pearson was ready for a new challenge. There was pride in considerable progress, and some personal pain, sometimes the price of progress. The field of a new day had been ploughed and many seeds planted. Others would now come along to nurture the growth, mature the new organization, and harvest the later yields.

For Pearson, at least on some days, the undesired transition in his own professional life seemed like the worst of times. Several significant new ministry positions surfaced as attractive possibilities for him, but he felt no freedom to accept any of them. Even so, being a man of strong faith, he naturally looked ahead, seeking the news God surely had in store. What would come next was totally unclear. Whatever it would be, he was determined that it would not be a ministry that conflicted with those of Church of God Ministries, the organization he was leaving and the church fellowship he loved and through which he continued to be ordained to Christian ministry. Pearson was in a personal wilderness and feeling somewhat abandoned and without direction.

An invitation came for Pearson to speak at an ecumenical gathering near his Indiana home. The focus was on intercessory prayer, intervening with God for those in crisis. As a way of encouraging the Christian leaders who would hear him, and clearly allowing the Bible to minister to himself, he spoke about the Old Testament story of Joseph being thrown into a cistern by his jealous brothers and then sold into slavery. Experiences of this kind are common, and certainly known by Christian leaders who dare to risk for God in difficult circumstances. Pearson insisted that Genesis 37-50 is a good word for all who find themselves in deep, dark, and dangerous places. God's promise is clear: "Even though you intended to do harm to me, God intended it for good..." (Gen. 50:20).

It is seldom the case that church people deliberately seek to hurt anyone; it is just that personalities, mixed agendas, and complicated circumstances conspire together and manage to result in harm. But even then, Pearson went on to explain, God reigns, forgives, and opens new doors, allowing the surprising and good to emerge. And so it would be for Pearson himself, even on this occasion.

During this gathering on intercessory prayer, Pearson asked the ministers present to pray for him. Then he was approached by representatives of the nearby Pendleton Church of God. They asked, "Would you consider being our pastor?" Their pastor was retiring and obviously Pearson was in transition. The idea was not readily acceptable. After all, Pearson had been serving on the national stage and was at the prime of his ministry. Large churches would likely open to him if he were patient, and Pendleton was a small congregation quite different culturally from Pearson's west-coast upbringing. Time would tell. At least he agreed to visit and maybe even be an interim pastor while continuing to explore other options.

One of the spiritual lessons that Pearson was about to learn was that, whatever the big picture still unseen ahead, he needed personal healing – and it might come from an unexpected source. The idea of serving a small Christian congregation, he began to think, might be an ideal setting for the needed healing, and maybe for even more. As it would turn out, the lesser demands of a small congregation would provide the opportunity, time, and energy for envisioning and launching something else, something really big that was about to invade Pearson's mind and heart. During the months when a relationship with the Pendleton congregation was developing, so were other things.

While functioning as General Director for the Church of God (Anderson), Robert Pearson had built a strong relationship with key leaders of the large African-American constituency of the Church of God movement. A milestone meeting of the Ministries Council of Church of God Ministries had occurred in the summer of 2000 and happened to have been hosted by the National Association of the Church of God in West Middlesex, Pennsylvania – home of many African-American leaders and ministries within the larger Church of God movement. That Council meeting had been particularly painful for Pearson because of administrative issues not related to the African-American constituency. Then, having left his national post, the next annual camp meeting of the National Association was convening on its home grounds in western Pennsylvania. It would be another key time for Pearson, but more positive in nature than the earlier one.

Jeffrey Jenness, chief executive officer of the national Board of Pensions of the Church of God, and later to be a charter member of Horizon's board of directors and its treasurer, was planning to attend the 2001 National Association meeting. He invited Pearson and C. J. Plogger to go along. Plogger had been a youth pastor in California under Pearson's earlier ministry in that state. Jenness was sensitive to the fact that Pearson was hurting inwardly, and he also judged that Pearson might benefit from the chance to travel east and enjoy great fellowship with his friends, and, of course, relish the inspired preaching so characteristic of the West Middlesex campmeetings. What Jenness did not recall at the time was that the Council meeting the year before had been on those grounds and would bring back painful memories for Pearson. Even so, they went and it turned out to be both an emotional and healing time.

The African-American leaders embraced and honored Pearson warmly. During one service, ordained clergy were invited to the chancel area to be anointed with oil. Plogger recalls that he and Jenness were unsure about participating since they were only guests. But Pearson said, "Let's go, this is important." Plogger then watched Pearson being anointed. These were amazing moments of divine presence.

"It appeared," Plogger recalls, "as if Bob's whole countenance was altered. There was a new peace that had not been there before. He had been ministered to in an incredible manner." As Jenness recalls, "The time spent on Zion's Hill [West Middlesex, Pennsylvania] provided a release for Bob that allowed him to passionately pursue whatever God was planning for his future ministry." The divine plan would begin to unfold just days after that Pennsylvania camp meeting in early August, 2001.

An unexpected and quite dramatic opportunity came to Robert Pearson. While being courted to become the pastor of the Pendleton Church of God, he received another invitation. This one was to travel to Africa! It was an invitation full of destiny, far more than anyone involved could see at the time. Those destiny days came in late August, 2001.

On March 20, 2002, looking back, now with some perspective, Pearson would report this to the public through a local newspaper, the *Pendleton Times*: "I went to Africa last August to see what God is doing there. While I was there, I discovered what God is doing in me." And what was that? God was planting in his servant a determination "to turn one of our world's greatest tragedies into an opportunity for God's people to make a difference."

Emerging now was a divine vision. Over the horizon was coming a new Christian ministry. Making a difference in the midst of tragedy was the new challenge, and Africa was the new location. The difference would come through launching Horizon International, a Christian not-for-profit ministry that would seek to raise up, right out of the tragedy of the AIDS pandemic, a new generation of African Christians – one rescued child at a time.

The peace that had come over Pearson's face while being anointed at the West Middlesex, Pennsylvania, meeting now would gather substance and direction – a new identity, a fresh passion, an unanticipated Christian ministry. He had learned a key lesson. The core calling of any Christian minister is to be a true servant, one willing to give up security and notoriety for the sake of following Jesus Christ without reserve. This Pearson would do. He had done it before, but now Christ was leading in surprising and dramatic new directions.

Darkness on the Land: Pandemic!

It was in September, 2001, only days after Pearson's trip to Africa, that the numbers "9/11" came into the English language as a shorthand designation for disaster. On the eleventh day of the ninth month, the unthinkable had happened in New York City, Washington, D.C., and rural Pennsylvania. Terrorists had struck and struck hard. There was massive destruction, the dead numbered more than two thousand, and the nation was in shock. One story in particular gripped the world.

United Airlines flight 93 had left Newark, New Jersey, that day on its way to San Francisco. At the same time as other planes were being hijacked to carry out the carefully planned terrorism, flight 93 was taken over by four men and forced to turn around and head for Washington, D.C. Cell phone use from the plane informed some passengers about the planes that already were crashing into the Trade Center towers in New York. This convinced some aboard flight 93 that their plane probably was involved in a larger plot and was targeting either the White House or the Capitol building in Washington.

This impending tragedy just could not be allowed! Something decisive had to be done, and immediately. A few passengers aboard, knowing that their deaths were inevitable either way, decided to act. Over rural Pennsylvania came the words via a cell phone, "Let's roll!" Three passengers rushed toward the hijacked controls and the plane plummeted downward. At great personal sacrifice, a few people saw the coming disaster for their nation and acted decisively, putting their lives on the line to make a difference. They died; many others lived.

The whole world soon heard about this heroism, and heard it again and again as the horrible and amazing story unfolded. What was less dominating in public focus, however, was another disaster then in progress, one that dwarfed the tragedy of the terrorist attacks on the United States. On flight 93, a handful of men had stepped into the gap and made an important difference. To help address the bigger disaster, four other men were preparing to do the same. They would do so away from the bright lights of the media. Without any cheering from the public or money in the bank, these men said to each other, "With the help of God, and for the orphaned children of southern Africa, let's roll!"

And what was the bigger disaster? The numbers "9/11" were being dwarfed by the letters "AIDS" (Acquired Immunodeficiency Syndrome). This is a disease of the body's immune system caused by a human immunodeficiency virus (HIV). AIDS is characterized by the death of CD4 cells, an important part of the body's immune system, leaving the body vulnerable to life-threatening conditions such as infections and cancers. This killer disease was already devastating lives in many countries, and it was being especially deadly in southern Africa. Robert Pearson would see it and never be the same again.

Sub-Saharan Africa has about ten percent of the world's population, but now it also was home to more than sixty percent of all people living with HIV. It was where more than eighty percent of all the world's children under age fifteen were living with the disease. It was being called a "pandemic" because of its global impact. Clearly, it was by far the greatest medical horror of modern history, greater than the loss of life in the two world wars combined.

The numbers heard by Pearson on his 2001 African trip were staggering. In the country of South Africa alone, it was being estimated that there would be eight million AIDS orphans in eight years – *and there was no plan in place to care for them*. The infection rate was even higher in several neighboring countries. Some 17 million Africans were already dead – 17 million just since the late 1970s. Of these, about 3.7 million were children, with another 12 million children left orphans, adding up to a human disaster of unimaginable proportions! But the disaster was not just the huge numbers.

The affected children in southern and eastern Africa were suffering increasingly from neglect as their parents weakened and finally died. After the deaths, the children often were destitute and suffered exploitation and abuse. Even if orphans were fortunate enough to have extended families to step in and help, they typically were stigmatized by society because of their association with HIV/AIDS. The tragedy that had befallen their parents now began torturing them as well. Even if medicine, food, housing, and schooling were available to them, and usually they are not, shame, fear, and rejection were common and sometimes brutal. It was a devastating pandemic spreading darkness on the land. Pearson's heart was broken. The stage was being set for something new.

A JOURNEY OF DESTINY

Robert Pearson's getting to Africa for this first time was surely God's doing. Here was more than a Christian leader experiencing a time of professional transition. He had taken initiative, actively networking in the Indianapolis area, hoping to find and assume some executive management position, maybe in the corporate rather than church world. But God had other ideas, intervening and sending this servant leader another way. This way would not be a new role in the secular world, but a new Christian ministry beyond his imagination, and beyond the boundaries of the United States.

The networking of Robert Pearson with a range of Christian executives began new friendships with leaders who would be important in his future ministry, and eventually that of Horizon International once it formally came into being. Included among these new friendships were ones with Brad Lindemann, Bill Freije, and Ethan Jackson. Later, Lindemann would introduce Pearson to Christine Herr who would become Mrs. Pearson in 2009. Freije would later comment on his first meeting with Pearson, sometime in 2000: "I remember being drawn to him. He was transitioning and humble enough to be very open about it – no games playing. Once he had been to Africa, he called to tell me about his dramatic experiences there, and the vision God had given him, and I chose to become involved."

Ethan and Joyce Jackson

That dramatic trip of destiny came about as follows. One morning in June, 2001, Pearson had a breakfast conversation in Indianapolis with Ethan Jackson, the executive of a consortium of companies called Basic American Industries. Ethan and his wife Joyce are committed Christians with strong interest in the mission of Jesus Christ, particularly in Africa. They also are generous supporters of select Christian ministries. Coming to understand Pearson's transitional circumstance, Christian commitment, and leadership potential, Ethan Jackson invited Robert Pearson to accompany him and others on an upcoming trip to Africa. All expenses would be paid! It would be a time of learning and exploration, and, as it turned out, it would be much more.

This unexpected generosity seemed to have destiny enfolded in it. Once in South Africa, Pearson met the Jackson's son, Kyle, in the university city of Stellenbosch near Capetown. Kyle was there in relation to the International Sports Leadership School led by Cassie Carstens, a significant Christian leader who hosted the visiting group and escorted them around the area. Kyle was honeymooning

Mary Beth and Kyle Jackson

with his new bride Mary Beth, daughter of Dr. Gene Habecker, a leader in Christian higher education back in the United States. Pearson had no way of knowing what all was ahead – including six years later the new Mrs. Jackson becoming a member of the board of directors of a new ministry he then would be leading. It would be called Horizon International.

Such things were yet unimaginable. For now, the task was to look and listen, taste and feel, wonder and learn about the future.

Robert Pearson meets and loves the children

While most of the learning would be sobering, even heartbreaking, a little of it was actually funny. Pearson knew what HIV/AIDS was in general, but he was not particularly aware of all of its physical manifestations. During a visit with a group of apparently healthy and fun-loving children, mostly intended as a time to relax and have some photos taken, Pearson noticed one little girl with colored spots on her tongue. This concerned him. He asked Jenny Carstens, wife of Cassie and a nurse, to look at the girl and see if the problem in her mouth might be from AIDS. Jenny looked carefully and then began laughing.

What could be funny about a possible case of AIDS? The humor was that the little girl had been coloring with a range of crayons and sticking  them in her mouth, making little spots like a dotted rainbow! She was as healthy as a three-year-old could be. If only that were the case with so many others not far away. The little girl smiled and held up one finger, a gesture captured in a photograph taken by Michael Henderson. He is an international church leader who was visiting these children with Pearson. This photo later birthed the idea of a slogan for the new Horizon International ministry. It would be a ministry of saving "one child at a time." And there were plenty needing to be saved. Horizon would be a ministry of turning pain, loneliness, and desperation into smiles of love, family, and fresh hope. All that, however, is getting ahead of the story.

Once in the shantytowns, the sprawling black townships scattered around Capetown, South Africa, Pearson began witnessing much more than fun-loving and healthy children at play. He saw what he later would describe as the "terrible scourge," "the gargantuan tragedy" of HIV/AIDS, including the waves of helpless orphans left in its ugly wake. His heart began to melt, and his mind began to search for answers. A trip made possible by the generosity of the Jacksons was becoming more of a pilgrimage to a life of new Christian ministry. Pearson now knew what he had to do. He must go home and find a way to do something about this human tragedy, even if only to save one child at a time!

A troubling question began pressing itself forward in the face of the alarming fact that at least 20% of South Africa's population was thought to be infected with HIV. It was put to Robert Pearson by Cassie Carstens, a local Christian leader he had just met: "How can South Africa build a country, post-apartheid, when the generation that should be in leadership is dying from HIV/AIDS?"

Two other questions were posed in Pearson's hearing by a Presbyterian church planter during Pearson's tour of a medical clinic in Capetown's Gugulethu township. They were even more troubling and presented a moral dilemma that a serious Christian could hardly ignore. Pearson began to be haunted by them. These questions were to become the seeds of the future for him.

With the very large number of orphans multiplying dramatically because of AIDS deaths in South Africa, the first question was posed by the minister. "Should we let the babies of our country live or die?" Pearson, stunned by the question, replied, "Of course you have to let them live. You at least have to try!" Then came the second question. "If we do help them to live, who is going to care for them?" There had to be an answer. Pearson offered his own response to Joyce Jackson as they left that clinic.

"Joyce, the church has a moral and ethical responsibility to turn this genocidal Good Friday into an Easter Sunday morning of joy a generation from now – one child at a time!" After all, Jesus had emerged from the grave that first Easter by the power of God; so the children of Africa now must be enabled to rise from the graves of their parents, again, only by the power of God. They just must!

Pearson's visit to Gugulethu was life-changing for him. Mary Beth Jackson recalls the visiting group arriving in a white Mercedes – it felt like the awkward "parading" of rich Americans. She recalls that Cassie Carstens had arranged this occasion and transportation to help the visitors sense the "huge gap" that exists in South Africa between wealth and poverty. Mary Beth had no idea at the time how deeply this experience was impacting one member of the group, Robert Pearson. It would become very clear to her later.

This township called Gugulethu is home to some 200,000 members of the Xhosa tribe. It is a place where the HIV/AIDS infection rate was nearing 40%. While there, Pearson and the others had entered the little dwelling of a man on his AIDS deathbed. His female partner was already dead from the same dreaded cause. After praying by the bedside, Pearson had walked into the hungry and bewildered little arms of their three children, all under five years old. He looked around and asked the obvious question. However, no one could tell him what would happen to these children. They probably would be short-lived orphans, virtual non-persons existing alone, always desperate in a dangerous and deprived world. Those three little faces began breaking Pearson's heart and disturbing his conscience wherever he went. God was speaking, calling Pearson to do something. Such children could not be left to their awful fate. Jesus had gently called such little ones to himself. Faithful disciples of the Master had to do the same – somehow.

This first trip to southern Africa happened for Robert W. Pearson in August, 2001. He had seen for himself and come home numbed by the immensity of the problem – and feeling called by God to become part of the solution. But what could he do? He had so little to work with, and the problem in Africa was larger than the most expansive imagination.

Pearson kept thinking of his personal encounter in 1978 with Mother Teresa and her Center for the Dying in Calcutta, India. If God were still on his throne, and if God does love "the least of these," then there had to be hope somewhere on the horizon. Maybe that hope was partly Pearson's responsibility to bring about. Not being able to get away from this conclusion, he determined to act. It was like God turning his nerves into steel and enabling him to face impossible odds. Like those brave men on that hijacked flight over Pennsylvania, Pearson declared, "Let's roll!"

He had made his decision – or God had made it for him. Robert Pearson would launch a new Christian ministry on behalf of the millions of desperate African children, a ministry of hope for otherwise hopeless children. It would have "horizon" in its name. Light must arise. A new day must dawn. The goal would be to create a world of hope for AIDS orphans, like the three kids he had left behind in Gugulethu (for whom it might already be too late). If not for them, he knew that there were millions more. Like the little girl with colors on her tongue and her one finger raised, there must be a Christian ministry of saving one child at a time.

THE AMAZING DREAM

Samuel G. Hines (1929-1995) was a big man. More than being substantial in physical presence, he had big visions and a huge Christian heart dedicated to reconciliation among God's children – people of all colors and in all nations. He insisted that people were born for relatedness, and his ministry was a sustained rebuke of any divisiveness that ruined human relationships. Originally from Jamaica and a Church of God (Anderson) pastor in Detroit and then Washington, D.C., beginning in 1969, Hines worked vigorously for racial harmony. He was deeply burdened with the institutionalized racism that prevailed for decades in South Africa after 1948. This preacher/leader confronted the evil of apartheid with a biblical passion, traveling often to South Africa to provide inspiration, build bridges of understanding among diverse cultural and political groups, and open doors to a better future.

Hines and his ministry were well known to Church of God leaders like Robert Pearson, Barry Callen, and Jeffrey Jenness – all of whom were about to continue his God-inspired work in a way they had not anticipated. Pearson in particular would benefit from this great ministry of yesterday. With apartheid now legally ended, the big need was to save a generation

Samuel G. Hines

24

of young Africans, who then could build a new and better South Africa. But how could this be done? The answer would involve an experience never to be forgotten by Pearson.

There is an old saying – "Life is not measured by the number of breaths we take, but by the moments that take our breath away." Robert Pearson was in for a breath-taking moment. Even if only a dream, it seemed so real – and it was so significant!

One night in May, 2001, at some level of sleepy unconsciousness when resistance was down and rationalizing was not active, Pearson saw himself standing in a body of water, just standing there a little bewildered. It wasn't so deep as to threaten danger; it was just calm water endlessly stretching in all directions. The isolation was oppressive and disorienting. There were no signs of life or land or hope. There was nothing – except water. Pearson was in a difficult time of transition in his life, having no idea where he was going next – maybe nowhere. He was adrift, anchored to nothing, just standing there, painfully, quietly, all alone. His heart was crying out to God, hoping that at least God was somewhere and could hear him in his lostness.

Time seemed to stand still as this searching man just stood in the midst of all this water. Then there was a small stirring in the water behind him that gently broke the empty silence. It was Jesus! Had the Master come rushing up to Pearson, walking miraculously on the water? No, he was just standing there, now in the water too, a divine presence in the midst of the hardest stuff of life. It was the gracious God who maybe had been there all the time, but just not noticed before. The timing or manner of God's arrival didn't matter. What mattered was what Jesus said.

"Bob," said Jesus, "I know you want to know what's on the horizon of your life. I have come to remind you of something you already know. I want you to make Me your horizon. If you will follow where I lead, you will always have the necessary light to guide your way. I will give you the light needed for your walking into the future, enough light for one step at a time." Jesus went on to explain that there was no need to look forward with a paralyzing anxiety. As long as Bob made the Lord the horizon of his life, the promise was that at least the next step to be taken would always be seen clearly.

Pearson awakened from this dream with these words of scripture on his heart and mind – "walk by faith, not by sight" (2 Cor. 5:7). The word "horizon" was somehow now a part of him and his future. From that dream conversation in the water with Jesus in May, 2001, came the August anointing at West Middlesex, Pennsylvania, and then the trip to Africa later the same month. And from all this would come a new horizon for desperate children. The point was to keep Jesus and his saving ministry as the first priority, then much would follow for the orphaned children.

The light that needed to rise over the horizon faced the immense blackness of the HIV/AIDS pandemic, likely the worst humanitarian crisis in the history of the human race. Numbers were hardly dependable (probably too low). In 2001, official reports said that there were 12.1 million African children under fourteen who were orphaned by AIDS. That number would be 14.2 million by 2005. Overwhelming! Any dealing with it would be against impossible odds – unless God was at the heart of the ministry equation. And God would be! After all, those kids, those desperate and often abandoned kids, apparently the least of God's creation, were children deeply loved by God.

Something had to be done! God wanted it done, and God's resources somehow would make the difference. The odds for success appeared impossible. It was like the great baobab tree of Africa. It can store large

The great baobab tree of Africa

amounts of water in its massive trunk and survive harsh drought conditions. Now this pandemic and flood of orphans overwhelmed mere man. Even so, God's resources were more than adequate.

God was already preparing the way. Robert Pearson first met Cassie and Jenny Carstens in August, 2001, when he was traveling in South Africa with Ethan and Joyce Jackson. They had attended a graduation in Capetown. It was a ceremony staged by the International Sports Leadership School, a Christian training camp for sports ministers from many nations. In addition to his involvement with this school,

Cassie and Jenny Carstens

Cassie Carstens was the chaplain for some 2,500 college students on the campus of the University of Stellenbosch, a Dutch Reformed school near Capetown that dates back into the nineteenth century – it had evolved into Victoria College in 1887 and then became the University of Stellenbosch in 1918. Cassie's wife Jenny was a hospice nurse in the city of Stellenbosch. She was feeling called to become involved in some form of AIDS-related ministry.

Maybe the Carstens could be part of the answer to the questions haunting Robert Pearson. He and the Carstens had connected – it seemed by divine appointment. A vision was being born. Were the odds of meaningful ministry in such dire circumstances really impossible? No, they were not. They couldn't be with God on the scene. It was time to join Joseph of old. Yes, it might be the worst of times, but, somehow, God could make it the best of times! A new ministry was about to be born.

Timothy Kumfer

Chapter Two

ONE CHILD AT A TIME

It could only start one way. A new ministry intended to address the disaster of millions of orphaned children had to begin with a vision of God's calling. A gigantic task would require divine resources. It also would take a gathering of gifted and generous ministry partners dedicated to the task. These partners would have to make clear their convictions and general strategy, and they would have to form an organizational framework through which the ministry could proceed. Starting from nothing, and in the face of a pandemic and a mountain of challenges stretching anyone's imagination, it would have to be one step, one partner, and one child at a time. And so it was that Horizon began.

A dream is only a dream unless it can find hands and feet to make it real. For any significant level of success, Robert W. Pearson's dream of bringing hope to the orphaned children of southern Africa would need resources almost beyond imagination, and many partners who would come to share the dream and lend their hearts, hands, dollars, contacts, and expertise to the massive task. It also would require more than everything human, more than the gifts of any group of people that could be found and focused on the task.

If a new ministry were not a "God thing," it would add up to very little. After all, that was the heart of Pearson's personal dream – make the lordship of Jesus the priority and his ministry to the desperate children would somehow follow. The first priority would always have to be put first.

God's direct intervention and gracious resourcing were necessary and prayerfully sought. After all, this sea of orphaned children was loved by God. So, the question was obvious. With God's help, how could a few Christians in the United States become effective agents of God's love in the lives of the desperate and dying so far away? If God would raise up partners in both the United States and Africa, maybe together they could submit to Christ's lordship, state their beliefs and driving motivations, create an organizational structure through which they could function, and identify specific strategies for transforming a God-inspired dream into practical reality.

Beginning at the opening of a new millennium in human history, the process of launching a new ministry for African orphans was envisioned and actually begun. Just as needed, divine resources began to appear. That was a God thing! So was Horizon International.

A CHURCH, BOARD, AND AFRICAN PARTNERS

Robert W. Pearson purchased a rural Indiana home in late 1998, soon after he had left a major ministry in California and had become the General Director of Church of God Ministries located in Anderson, Indiana. Since the home was located near the town of Pendleton in central Indiana, and he hoped to remain in it following his ministry as General Director, the Church of God (Anderson) congregation in

Church of God, Pendleton, Indiana

Pendleton was conveniently located and had come to his attention. The timing was right for a relationship to develop between them.

Pearson was a guest at this Pendleton congregation on February 11, 2001, being introduced by Rev. Clarence Phairas who was ending his pastoral ministry there. Pearson preached at the church on March 18, and soon after accepted an invitation to be the interim pastor. Then in August, while visiting Africa for the first time with Ethan and Joyce Jackson, the congregation formally called him to be its pastor. From an internet café in Stellenbosch near Capetown, Pearson emailed his willingness to serve as senior pastor. His ministry vision was stretching from the small town of Pendleton, Indiana, to human needs and service opportunities across the United States and far beyond. For now, however, he would return from Africa and base his personal ministry in Pendleton.

Todd Faulkner joined him in Pendleton as the associate minister. Faulkner was a creative and committed young man completing his ministerial education at the nearby Anderson University campus. In the years ahead, both this congregation and its associate minister, and his wife, Cindy Faulkner, would join Robert Pearson in the fast-growing new ministry that soon would be called Horizon International. The members of this congregation had begun hearing from their pastor about his new experiences in Africa and his growing ministry vision for the many orphaned children there. Something new, something important was about to be birthed.

Todd and Cindy Faulkner

The month of August, 2001, became a milestone. Pastor Pearson was carrying on his new duties at the small Pendleton congregation and had made his life-changing first trip to Africa. Upon his return to the United States, he prayed much, consulted with several trusted people, and made a big decision. He would launch a new African orphan ministry from his modest base in Pendleton, Indiana. Only a determined visionary with unusual energy and administrative skills could reasonably attempt such a thing. He was such a man, and he was determined, but it could not be done alone.

Pearson began by communicating regularly with his new friends, the Carstens in South Africa. Since he needed African partners, he did the obvious thing. He invited the Carstens to join his new faith venture. They were open to the possibility, retreated for prayer and reflection on their own ministries, and soon decided that God was in favor of them linking in some manner with whatever Pearson would create in the United States. So far, this proposed partnership was little more than a gleam in the eye and a fire in the soul of one American minister. Even so, Pearson was a natural entrepreneur and networker of people, and the Carstens were much the same, and they had excellent contacts in the church, medical, and even political communities of South Africa and beyond.

D. Michael Henderson

It was not long before Robert Pearson made his bold move organizationally. The Carstens had agreed to be African partners, and Pearson began meeting with D. Michael Henderson, a key local contact provided by Ethan Jackson. Henderson, a former missionary in Kenya with World Gospel Mission, now headed the organization *Heart of Africa* based in Greenwood, Indiana. He was pleased to give Pearson valuable information on how to start a not-for-profit corporation in Indiana. With these resources in hand, Pearson then turned to three dear friends, asking each if he would be willing to serve as a charter member of the board of directors of a new ministry organization he was forming. While they had a range of significant gifts to resource such an organization, he made it clear that they would have to proceed on faith since they would be pioneering a ministry from the ground up.

One of these men was Eric Dwiggins, a businessman in the Pendleton congregation being pastored by Pearson. He was the operational manager for the area's distribution of Car Brite supplies, and he was a man who did not like meetings and was not inclined to join governing boards of anything, including his own local church. Even more, he thought that helping children in Africa was impractical and likely an ill-conceived idea – they were so far away, after all, and so

Jenny and Cassie Carstens

many children much closer home really needed help too. Dwiggins also pondered the thought that the major spread of AIDS in southern Africa was largely the fault of the Africans themselves (spread by sexual contact) – so, did these children deserve massive assistance over others much closer to home who were "innocent" of causing their own problems? The children themselves, of course, had not caused the problem, but the irresponsible adults around them had.

Such questions were shared by many in the United States and provided caution. Even so, mostly to help his pastor and friend, Dwiggins agreed to serve on the new board of directors (probably for just a year or so). He did not really share Pearson's passionate vision, but that would soon change! His questions did have good answers.

The second new board member was Barry L. Callen, a Church of God minister, former vice-president for academic affairs of Anderson University, former dean of that university's seminary when Pearson was a student there, and a scholar and professional editor and writer. While he had often traveled around the world, sometimes leading student groups from the university who were sacrificing to support the Christian mission, Callen had no previous contact with the AIDS pandemic and, other than one trip to Kenya in the 1980s, had no experience in Africa. He also came to the board with more questions than vision, but he had known Pearson since the 1970s and had faith in him as a Christian leader. Callen was ready to risk, have faith, and lend his skills to a new Christian venture.

The third new board member was Jeffrey A. Jenness, another national leader of the Church of God movement, serving as chief executive officer of the Board of Pensions of the church – a very

Eric Dwiggins   *Barry L. Callen*   *Jeffrey A. Jenness*

responsible and demanding position. He also knew and believed in Pearson and was willing to bring his financial expertise and loving Christian spirit to the new board's membership. He would bring a disciplined realism in finance, along with his enthusiasm for the Christian cause, especially when related to desperate children. Jenness labored every day on behalf of retired Christian leaders in North America. He now was inspired by the possibilities of assisting a new generation of Christian leaders to emerge in Africa.

That was it – these three men joining Pearson to comprise the complete membership of the founding board of directors of Horizon International. These four men all lived within a few miles of each other in central Indiana and were willing to give guidance to this new ministry. As they first looked at each other around a table and realized the need to form a corporation with established officers, choices were few and obvious. Pearson was named president, Dwiggins vice-president, Callen corporate secretary, and Jenness treasurer. The group was small, but there was clear competence in every post, and there was obvious determination and hope that this new ministry would make a difference through hard work, careful choices, the generosity of many people, and the wisdom and power of God's Spirit. While fragile and barely a reality, Horizon International had begun and had a wonderful future ahead, one that stretched well beyond the imaginations of its founding board members.

Barry Callen and Jeffrey Jenness had stood by Pearson as compassionate supporters during his emotionally demanding time of transition from the General Directorship of Church of God Ministries. They now agreed to stand by him as he transitioned into what promised to be a major new ministry. Neither of them at the time had any idea just how major it would be! Dwiggins stood by the new president as a layperson supportive of the Pendleton congregation's growing encouragement of a new world venture being headed by its pastor. Later, he would admit with a grin on his face that he had not been particularly comfortable at first with these two "eggheads from Anderson" (Callen and Jenness). No matter. Dwiggins brought to the board some unique experience and practical wisdom that the others quickly recognized and appreciated. The four men learned to know and love each other. They were Christian brothers, and now fellow adventurers of a divine journey.

All members of the new board of directors agreed to serve as fellow travelers on a largely unknown journey. They brought to the board's table quite a range of expertise and a deep commitment to Jesus Christ and his mission in this world. It would be a faith venture, one starting from scratch. The intent was not to form a "Church of God" organization, despite the affiliations of the board members. It was to be a ministry of the *whole body of Christ*. In fact, the board would be particularly careful not to become a competitor with the mission enterprise of the church body with which they all were affiliated – one as a layperson and the other three as ordained ministers.

These four men, the beginning board members and corporate officers, all volunteers, rejoiced in their different gifts, recognized their own limitations, and reached out quickly for the help they needed. For instance, Pearson worked to get in motion the various documents and resolutions required to form a new Indiana corporation, including having an attorney friend, Wesley D. Schrock, draft a proposed set of bylaws, which soon was approved. Secretary Callen began keeping detailed minutes of all board meetings and a cumulative listing of all resolutions and actions of the board of directors. Things had to be done carefully, responsibly, and consistently. Integrity had to mark every move made.

First Horizon Board of Directors
L. to R.: Eric Dwiggins, Robert Pearson, Jeffrey Jenness, and Barry Callen

D. Michael Henderson, a friend of Barry Callen for many years and now a new friend of Robert Pearson, was consulted. His great spirit and extensive mission experience as executive director of the ministry Heart of Africa soon became an invaluable resource of wisdom. Later, in May, 2007, Horizon's board of directors would formally acknowledge *Heart of Africa* "as one of our strategic partners." Of course, from the very beginning, the Carstens in South Africa were exceptionally significant partners in the new ministry enterprise that increasingly appeared to be divinely inspired. What was decided in Indiana had practical significance only when partners "on the ground" in Africa put their hearts and hands to the hard work of actual implementation.

Back in the United States, Pearson shared his ministry vision with a widening circle of dear friends of many years, several of whom lived on the West Coast where he had grown up and ministered. Among these friends were Larry and Joyce Hartman from California. They had known Pearson since his pastoral years, and especially from his years of leading the cooperative ministries of the Church of God in southern California. The Hartmans were both members of the Garden Grove Church of God and professional educators with a heart for Christian mission. Occasionally, they had hosted in their home meetings of the area Christian Education Commission of the Church of God. In these meetings, there were many pizzas and much serious conversation about the work of God. In such meetings, the Hartmans had come to believe in Pearson's visionary gifts, obviously from God.

After the September 11, 2001, terrorism attacks in New York City and elsewhere, the Hartmans visited Indiana and their special friend, Robert Pearson. He shared with them his new call from God for the African orphans and his dream of a new ministry organization. They believed in him and immediately wanted to help, becoming one of the very first donors – and they have remained regular donors ever since. Later, the Hartmans would help arrange housing when Horizon's Kuyasa Kids Choir would visit California on tour (see chapter five), and they would help arrange area gatherings on behalf of Horizon so that the story could be shared with more and more people. After years of such involvement, this would be their judgment: "We've been amazed at the stories Bob Pearson tells us of God's working through Horizon!"

For the Hartmans, and for many others, involvement with what would be Horizon International began with the presence, enthusiasm, commitment, and personal credibility of one man, Robert Pearson, a man they knew well and trusted unreservedly. He turned to such people, telling the Horizon story, sharing his divine vision, and inviting their participation in the ministry.

Larry and Joyce Hartman

With proposed bylaws now in hand, Pearson called for the inaugural meeting of the new board of directors. It convened on November 7, 2001, in a restaurant in Anderson, Indiana, with the four founding directors present. The proposed set of bylaws for the new "Horizon Children's Homes International" was reviewed and approved by the directors. Attention was then turned to the formal election of corporation officers. According to the new bylaws, the corporation would have its principal offices in Pendleton, Indiana.

In the years to follow, the "Children's Homes" part of the corporate name would be dropped because it did not represent adequately the more complex ministry strategy soon to develop. The word "Horizon," however, was permanent. It had been chosen for two reasons. First, that amazing dream experienced by Robert Pearson had featured Jesus saying to him, "Bob, make me your horizon." Second, the symbol of hope in Africa is that of a rising sun. This image of light spreading and a fresh future dawning is the one that this new ministry hoped to convey and embody.

So, it had actually begun! At least, the modest skeleton of an organization was in place. The excitement was obvious, as was the irony. The inaugural board meeting on behalf of desperate children in southern Africa had happened in *Red Lobster* on Scatterfield Road in Anderson, Indiana, an upscale American restaurant with abundant food on all hands. The irony was not lost on the board members, but at the time there had been nowhere else to meet (no corporate office or board room existed). The driving hope was that the evident richness of North America could be harnessed and shared elsewhere with those so much less fortunate.

The first formal report of the Horizon president to the board was delivered in that inaugural meeting. It spoke of the reign of God in Jesus Christ, from which all Christian beliefs and ministries flow. The new Horizon ministry, president Pearson said, was dedicated to addressing one of the more pressing humanitarian needs ever to face the world – surely a ministry effort in full accord with the present intent of the reign of Jesus Christ. He recalled with deep appreciation the rich heritage of the ministry of reconciliation carried on in South Africa by the now-deceased Samuel G. Hines, beloved Church of God (Anderson) minister. He noted that Sam's wife, Dalineta, had been apprised of this new faith venture in Africa. He also had reported her response.

"My late husband," Mrs. Hines had said, "would have been enthusiastically supportive!" Sam, and many others in that "great cloud of witnesses," watched as their own Christian passion was now going forth into the world by the hands of a new group of Christ's servants.

Pearson's first report to the new board of directors went on to recall his recent travel to South Africa and to state that Cassie and Jenny Carstens were prepared to provide operational leadership for Horizon in that country. While dollars to make all this possible were still only a dream, it was a big dream, and he was convinced that it was being inspired by God. Thus, the board should be confident that ways would be found to move forward. In fact, in this first board meeting, a proposed corporation budget for 2002 was presented and approved. It was a budget of $250,000!

Since there was no history of this ministry's potential income or required expenditures, such a budget was certainly a bold faith venture. All agreed that money would be spent only as it actually came in. Integrity would be crucial. Pearson would work at fundraising, and already had mailed donor letters to 150 of his family members and personal friends. He also would be flying back to South Africa on November 23 with Michael Henderson to cement the partnership with the Carstens and identify a strategic site for the first orphan project of Horizon. Henderson was experienced in such matters and offering valuable assistance.

The vision and determination were clear. A modest sense of the most appropriate mission strategy was emerging. The president of the new Horizon ministry ended his first formal report to the board of directors with this: "Should we let the babies die? Christ would compel us to help them live! If we encourage them to live, who is going to care for them? With your guiding oversight, *we* will!"

A fortunate fact was now becoming clear. Robert Pearson's congregation in Pendleton, Indiana, was increasingly aware of this international vision of its pastor, and of the new organization just formed. As its awareness grew, it was open to being caught up in it with him. One of the founding board members of Horizon was Eric Dwiggins, a layperson in the church. Sally Bramley, soon to be the church secretary, became one of the first North American sponsors of an African child through Horizon. Others quickly followed. In August, 2003, Horizon was formally added to the congregation's mission budget at a level of one percent of the general budget, and the commitment was later increased to $2,500 annually, a major amount for a small congregation.

Pearson was committed to his pastoral role. Nonetheless, it would become more difficult to be both a pastor and president, especially one having to travel internationally on occasion. He remained the senior pastor in Pendleton until May, 2004. By then, Horizon's ministry had grown so large and demanding of his time as president that a decision would become necessary. He would leave the pastorate, with his associate, Todd Faulkner, assuming the senior role.

Such leadership continuity was fortunate for the stability of the church. Pearson would remain a layperson in the church for another four years, although he would be gone much of the time traveling for Horizon. The Pendleton congregation had been all that he had hoped – a good place of divine service where his own healing could occur, and, as it turned out, also a base from which he could manage to launch an even broader base of ministry. Horizon would always be in debt to this fine body of Christian people.

The Way Ahead: A Ministry Strategy

What was the best way to proceed in moving Horizon from the dream stage to being an effective instrument in God's hands? The first moves in the life of any new ministry organization tend to bring a host of perplexing questions, and they seem to come all at once.

It would take the collective wisdom of all the partners in the new Horizon venture to find the best paths to walk. By good fortune – or, more likely, by God's guiding hand, in late 2001 the Carstens from South Africa were scheduled to be in Jamaica for a meeting of the International Sports Coalition, an organization in which Cassie served as board chair. They were willing to spend the extra time necessary to fly to Indianapolis, Indiana, to share in a day of strategic thinking about Horizon's future. The headquarters of the Free Methodist Church in North America is near the Indianapolis airport. One of its conference rooms was made available for this critical meeting on November 12, 2001. Cassie and Jenny Carstens met with the newly elected president and secretary of Horizon, Robert Pearson and Barry Callen. Present also were consultants Michael and Martha Henderson.

Evident already was the deliberate ecumenical and multi-cultural nature of the Horizon venture. Two Church of God (Anderson) ministers – Callen and Pearson – were meeting in the headquarters of

God was gathering ministry leaders from across the Body of Christ and around the world - hope was on the horizon!

L. to R.: Barry Callen, Jenny and Cassie Carstens, Robert Pearson, Michael and Martha Henderson

the Free Methodist Church with a Dutch Reformed ordained minister and chaplain and his wife Jenny, and with consultant Michael Henderson, a United Methodist minister, and his wife Martha, leaders long associated with World Gospel Mission. Horizon was to be a ministry representing the whole Christian community in sacrificial service to a world of desperately needy children. It would proceed through a careful process of dialogue in search of informed wisdom.

This day's conversation in November, 2001, was an important milestone on the way to Horizon's future. It soon was agreed that child sponsorships would be developed by recruiting North American monthly donors. The question then was whether it would be best to use this money for placing children in traditional orphanages, the "children's homes" phrase in the original name of the new ministry. The group's sentiment was that orphanages tend to create sterile cultures where children are cut off from traditional families and communities. The better alternative seemed to be community-based central facilities that would provide food, clothing, education, medical attention, and counseling, with the children placed in nearby Christian foster homes supervised and serviced by Horizon staff from the central base.

Here was the beginning of a ministry model to build on. It was understood, however, that as experience came and multiple cultural settings for ministry emerged, the model would be adapted as local needs, leadership, and ministry wisdom dictated. Both new South African townships and provinces, and even new African countries, would soon become part of Horizon's future. The many differences involved would require a constant reassessment of precise policies and procedures for appropriate ministry. The president and members of the board of directors accepted the related requirements of patience and flexibility on their part.

This crucial and formative dialogue in Indianapolis was followed rather quickly by Robert Pearson and his consultant friend Michael Henderson returning to South Africa from November 25 to December 1, 2001 – a time that later would be called by Pearson a "God-anointed week!" This trip had three purposes, all of which would be accomplished.

One purpose of this trip was to further cement Horizon's working relationship with the Carstens. This was accomplished. In fact, Cassie Carstens soon resigned his chaplaincy of the large student church at Stellenbosch University to concentrate on the International Sports Leadership School and be Horizon's point person in South Africa. He would function as a passionate reconciler and relational networker, lifting up the vision for community transformation through AIDS orphan ministry. His salary would be provided through donations from the South African Christian business community.

Jenny Carstens, Cassie's wife and a gifted organizer and experienced hospice nurse, would be central to the actual work of Horizon in South Africa. She would work at getting Horizon's first ministry project identified and off the ground. Funding was soon secured from the North Coast Calvary Chapel in Carlsbad, California, and other donors to enable Jenny to be Horizon's first full-time staff partner in southern Africa.

A second purpose of this African trip was research and education. Pearson and Henderson visited the Stellenbosch Hospice and the Stellenbosch AIDS Action Center, meeting staff, discussing the local needs, and identifying organizations already seeking to address them. Then these two men and Jenny Carstens visited the Christian AIDS Bureau in the nearby city of Wellington. They learned there that the AIDS infection rate in the black townships in the Capetown area was about 36%, and that advertising a new ministry as "AIDS orphans" could carry an unwanted community stigma among local populations. This was important information. Wisdom includes being sensitive to local perceptions of the motives and strategies of an "outside" organization.

A third purpose of this African trip in late 2001 was to follow up on the November 12 strategy meeting in Indianapolis. Michael Henderson and Robert Pearson met with area pastors, Christian leaders who knew life in the townships at close hand and whose help would be crucial for effective ministry there. The central question posed to the pastors was, "How can Horizon best care for AIDS orphans in the Stellenbosch/ Capetown area?" It soon became clear that the particular township called Kayamandi was the likely place for Horizon to begin. Pastors there would have ownership of the new effort and would assist in crucial ways.

On Tuesday, November 27, Cassie and Jenny Carstens convened a group of ten Christian pastors from Stellenbosch and Kayamandi to meet with them and Robert Pearson. From them, Pearson learned that the AIDS infection rate in Kayamandi was about 40%. This alarmingly high rate caused one pastor to comment, "In twenty years people won't be fighting over land to live on, but space to bury their dead!" All agreed that Kayamandi was the right place for Horizon to begin. And what was the best model for the beginning? That key question dominated the conversation of the Americans and Africans who were preparing to partner in Christian ministry.

Early meeting of Robert Pearson and South African pastors

The pastors said that Horizon should build one or two multipurpose community centers housing support services for orphans who should be placed in Christian homes in the Kayamandi community – –with the children supported by sponsorships from North America through Horizon. The pastors were ready to assist in finding the homes and the children that Horizon then could screen and select. Horizon would search in North America for people who would be willing to provide the necessary funding on a monthly basis. With all doing their part, hope could begin to shine over the horizon in the diseased darkness of Kayamandi.

This consultation with African pastors, happening at the very beginning of the life of Horizon International, signaled a central commitment of the new ministry. Horizon's intention would be to "create a world of hope for AIDS orphans." It would not be merely another humanitarian effort to help with the physical needs of young Africans – needed and worthy as any such effort is. Horizon would be a distinctly *Christian* ministry, a healing initiative of the Body of Christ in concert with a broad range of Christian leaders and always in dialogue with the best local wisdom.

Eventually, the time would come when the board of directors of Horizon would address formally the core issue of defining Horizon's mission. In its December 6, 2008, meeting, the board declared for the record what had been the case from the beginning. Horizon was and intended always to be a church-related orphan care ministry, a Christ-centered organization in active partnership with local African individuals and churches of varying Christian traditions, as opposed to being merely another source of humanitarian aid for its own sake and apart from the larger mission of the Body of Christ.

Therefore, the task was more than rescuing children from premature deaths. While supplying all necessary life support and loving care to the orphans it would serve, Horizon's larger vision would be to raise up a new generation of African Christians ready to serve the future needs of their nations. Feed, house, clothe, and educate the children, of course; but also, Horizon would nurture the spirits of the children, bringing hope, filling their minds with wisdom, and opening their souls to the transforming grace of God in Jesus Christ. These basic commitments and central beliefs of Horizon are explored further in chapter three.

Meaning often is captured best in nicknames and symbols. Over the years to come, Horizon's traveling groups from North America, once safely home, would make a common observation about Horizon's president. They would say: "People don't really know Robert Pearson unless they have traveled with him in Africa and witnessed his unbridled passion and joy as he relates to the orphaned children." The African kids call him "Uncle Bob." It would be so obvious that he loves the children unreservedly, and they would find delightful ways of showing that this love was very mutual. When with them, he would seem to function in some sacred zone all his own.

On one occasion in Harare, Zimbabwe, the kids would give him a gift just before lunch, something precious to them, part of some future meal not yet cooked. He would hold tightly this wiggling animal and listen with delight as they chanted, "Chicken Bob!" The loving connection between them was deep, sometimes funny, and usually marked by singing.

"Chicken Bob"

That chicken was a symbol of joy and love, a humorous gift from children being rescued from disaster, children who again had a family – Horizon. Alongside the chicken were more sober symbols, ones of the disaster itself. A particular one would move any compassionate heart. Before ending his second trip to South Africa, Robert Pearson and Michael Henderson attended an early morning AIDS Remembrance Service at a bridge over First River in the heart of downtown Stellenbosch. The highlight was throwing rose petals from the bridge into the moving water below, each petal representing a person who had died from AIDS in the last year.

Rose petal
AIDS remembrance

This was a truly moving experience for Pearson. He watched the water's pulsating surface coated with floral memories of the recent dead. As he gently dropped his petals, he reaffirmed in his heart that Horizon would do all it possibly could to minister to the many children being left behind by the HIV/AIDS scourge. It would serve as a burst of light in the dark night of death and desperation. Life would replace death, one child at a time!

Grassroots-Up DNA

Another dramatic symbol of the nature and mission of Horizon International would impact Timothy Kumfer very personally in 2005. He was pastoring the Big Lake Church of God in Columbia City, Indiana, and leading a work camp for Horizon. The visiting Americans were hard at work in the township of Bloekombos in South Africa's Western Cape, working on the construction of a community center. The shell of a large new building surrounded some old walls that needed removed, along with much "junk" which was being carried to the street and immediately was disappearing (junk to some is very valuable to someone else who has little in life). This process of disappearing junk was symbolic enough, but there was more.

As the old wall was brought down a piece at a time, a crowd gathered along the street outside the fence. They grew restless and even a little angry as they watched white people destroying something in their community, what they thought was the usual thing white outsiders did. Domination and destruction was all that they had ever known. Once Kumfer realized what was happening, and why, he helped get to the street a few local people who were working with the Horizon group. They explained to the crowd in their own language and cultural context what was really happening.

How important it was to have good communication. Horizon, the people must understand, was not another arrogant organization of whites doing what it judged best for poor people in Africa – and without their understanding or permission. Instead, local African leaders were to be full partners being empowered to guide in the development of their own future, with Horizon supportingly by their sides. Once this was understood, the crowd's mood lightened, even shifted toward the truly appreciative.

President Robert Pearson would make an important point in his presentation to Horizon's board of directors on September 8, 2007: "One of the secrets to our success in Africa," he would observe, "has been our grassroots-up organizational model." Before becoming a type of organization, however, this secret had been an underlying value and attitude consistently held by Horizon's leaders. This ministry would turn to local Christian leaders for wisdom on how best to proceed with ministry in their African localities. When the ministry path was mutually determined, qualified locals would be accepted as significant ministry leaders, with Horizon choosing to function more in a *partnering* and *empowering* than in a dictating role. Usually, Horizon would pay for filing to secure domestic non-profit status with the government, provide a significant share of the non-profit's funding, and welcome local leaders as guiding organizational leaders. It would play the servant's role – no fresh western colonialism here!

An early example of this empowerment model was the formation of *Kuyasa Horizon Empowerment* in Kayamandi township, Western Cape Province, South Africa. Soon there would be *Horizon Thusanang* in Limpopo Province, South Africa. These and others would be African legal entities, Horizon partners. Occasionally, Horizon would partner with existing non-profit organizations like *Sarfat* in Bloekombos township, Western Cape Province, South Africa, and the *Jehovah Jirah Trust* in Harare/MaShonaland, Zimbabwe. These bodies all have significant local leadership, supported by the enabling structure and outside funding of Horizon International.

The organizational approach of Horizon, typically and from its beginning, has been to "come alongside" African ministering partners. Such an approach has been called "grassroots-up" as opposed to the more domineering top-down style of organization and ministry. This manner of proceeding has been at the heart of Horizon's organizational DNA. It has been the approach even when, as later would be the case in Uganda,

Horizon registers formally with a government as a ministry in and of itself. Such a DNA has its inherent and obvious values – and its occasional and frustrating dilemmas.

Positively, this style of ministry – partnering with and empowering others – builds an intensity of ownership and participation by indigenous African leaders, and sometimes earns more respect and tolerance from African governments. Negatively, it is possible that this type of partnering can foster such a strong African identity with a ministry that the Africans seek independence from or even work at cross purposes with Horizon's mission. Regardless of this negative possibility, and opposed to the colonial memories in many nations of southern and eastern Africa, Horizon has chosen the empowerment path, and the rewards have been predominately positive.

Another key aspect of Horizon's organizational DNA is that it is a *body-of-Christ* ministry. Intentionally, it is not accountable to or defined and restricted by any one denominational group of Christians. This ecumenical approach is a clear advantage when working with city, township, or village pastors with a wide variety of denominational affiliations, or with none. Horizon has stated its own theological convictions, clearly Christian but not narrowly denominational (see chapter three). Accordingly, Horizon would soon develop close working relationships with indigenous church groups like the Eternal Church of God in southwest Uganda and the Eternal Word Ministries in Harare/MaShonaland, Zimbabwe. The issue is never the name of the group, but its clear Christian commitment and its willingness to serve accountably in partnership with Horizon on behalf of the desperate needs of orphaned children.

Some prominent Horizon leaders and consultants in Africa would have Dutch Reformed, Baptist, United Methodist, and Pentecostal backgrounds, and later developments would come to involve the Church of God (Anderson), particularly in the Lusaka and Livingston areas of Zambia. The Roman Catholic Church in 2006 would give *Horizon Thusanang* a major piece of land in Matipane Village, a former fairgrounds of the Sepedi tribe in South Africa. The only restriction of this gift would be that Horizon never refuse to sponsor an orphan because he or she were Roman Catholic – absolutely no problem for Horizon!

Another way to identify the distinctive organizational and missional DNA of Horizon is to note who is judged to be the ministry's "heroes." This would be highlighted on September 14, 2008, in California when Cindy Nixon, a Horizon staff missionary then serving in Capetown, South Africa, was being married to Neal de Beer. A woman referred to Robert Pearson, who was attending, as the "hero of Horizon." He pondered this high compliment during his flight back to Indiana. Yes, he was the founder and is the chief executive officer of Horizon, the person often found in the public spotlight. But that is only public prominence, hardly an adequate way of determining heroic ministry. So he decided to write a letter to Horizon donors that would single out two of the real ministry heroes in his opinion.

The October, 2008, donor letter, focused on two women. Sharon Parry by then was delivering food parcels to Horizon's twenty-one orphaned kids in Victoria Falls, Zimbabwe, sometimes at the risk of her own life. Pumla Antony was leading Horizon's care ministry in Bloekombos township in the Western Cape Province of South Africa. She was sharing her very life with Horizon's twenty-seven orphaned kids there. These are the true heroes, explained the letter, those who do the hard work with all their hearts and at significant personal cost. It surely was for people like Sharon and Pumla that Roger Whittaker wrote his song "Wind Beneath My Wings."

Sharon Parry

Pumla Antony

Pearson thought of himself, and then of these two Horizon women, and of several dozen others then laboring with Horizon in four countries in southern and eastern Africa. Then a few of the words of this Whittaker song came into his mind: "I can fly higher than an eagle, but you are the wind beneath my wings." There it was, the true story of heroic ministry. Those serving faithfully on the ground in Africa every day are the wind that drives all else. Servant thinking like this is central to the DNA of Horizon International!

Chapter Three

BELIEFS AND BEGINNINGS

One should not attempt to live the Christian life or engage in Christian ministry without (1) clear beliefs that are biblically informed and (2) a commitment to live out those beliefs with God's help. To have the proper roots in divine revelation is to be theologically grounded and God-directed; not to have such roots is a path to frustration, confusion, and probable disaster. Horizon International has stated clearly its beliefs, values, and motivations and strategies for ministry. It began in 2001 and has ministered ever since because of a divine calling and a proper understanding of the church's mission in today's troubled world. Very early, it established guidelines for setting ministry priorities and, in Kayamandi township in the Western Cape province of South Africa, it found the right place to begin the journey of living out its call.

Chapter two speaks of the "DNA" of Horizon International. It is a particular style of ministry, a servant attitude, a preference for "partners" instead of "employees," an empowerment approach to desperate orphans and ministry organizations in Africa. But Horizon is more. Its vision and corporate character are based on a particular set of values and theological beliefs that grow directly out of the Christian faith tradition. These values and beliefs stand on the whole of biblical revelation, reach out to the whole of God's people, and embrace with compassion the pressing needs of the least of God's creation – the orphaned children.

In brief, the vision and mission of Horizon International can be summarized and is to be publically declared as follows. Christian identity and ministry are based on recognition of the sovereign reign of God, through Jesus Christ, in the immediate presence, wisdom, and power of the Holy Spirit. Horizon gladly affirms this gracious reality and recognizes the AIDS-related plight of millions of children in southern and eastern Africa as an urgent concern of this triune and loving God.

Thus, Horizon's ministries exist to address this concern through providing direct assistance to such children in multiple ways, all under the inspiration of God's Spirit. Loving care for the desperate young can be a path to a future more like God intends. That better future would be for the children themselves, and later, through them, for their nations as the children mature in body and faith and find ways to make tomorrow different from today.

In Christian compassion, Horizon – as an interdenominational Christian ministry – seeks to serve "the least of these" in concert with a wide range of caring individuals, congregations, and organizations. Established in the United States in 2001, Horizon focuses its attention on the great need of so many of the young in southern and eastern Africa. It provides for the present with food, shelter, love, education, and medicine, and for the future with skill-training, higher education, and programs of community transformation. Since it does "take a village" to raise a child, Horizon seeks to address constructively the social and economic structures surrounding the children under its care.

LEAPING FROM THE STALL

As it gathered partners and child sponsors and launched its first orphan ministry projects in 2001 and 2002, Horizon International needed to be clear about its basic values, beliefs, and ministry commitments. There inevitably would be numerous opportunities and conflicting agendas brought to Horizon's table by a range of organizations and individuals. Decisions would require a clear eye and persistent discipline to keep Horizon from straying from God's appointed path. In the lead was Robert W. Pearson, a well educated and experienced Christian minister who was articulate about his personal beliefs and motivations. On the founding board of directors was Barry L. Callen, a widely published

Christian theologian who could give well-informed guidance. The Bible was to be open, understood, and followed. Right belief was never to be separate from necessary action.

In that November, 2001, milestone meeting in Indianapolis that helped set Horizon's early direction, Cassie Carstens of South Africa made a suggestion that was soon presented to the Horizon board of directors and enthusiastically affirmed. He suggested that Horizon adopt Malachi 4:2 as its theme Bible verse. It reads: "For you who revere my name, the sun of righteousness shall rise with healing in its wings. You shall go out leaping like calves from the stall" (NRSV).

This Bible verse was seen as carrying four keynotes that picture dramatically Horizon's core nature and divinely-determined purpose. They are:

1. Horizon leaders are committed Christians *who revere God's name.* The intent is to nurture AIDS orphans in a Christian environment that reverences God.

2. The Horizon organizational logo will be that of a rising sun since, for the orphans to be served, *the sun of righteousness will indeed rise.*

3. Horizon's care of AIDS orphans will include a Christian ministry dimension that will bring *healing in its wings.*

4. Raising up a new generation of Africans in a Christian environment will enable children, once hopelessly bound, to *go out and leap like calves released from the stall!*

These four ministry keynotes were to be joined together by an overarching principle. Horizon's mission is *to connect first-world resources with third-world expertise for the sake of the orphaned children of Africa.* This principle would be fleshed out in light of the following three strategic values. The AIDS orphan ministry of Horizon International must be. . .

1. *Attached to the local Christian community* – a cluster of community churches, a single large congregation, or a Christian organization.

2. *Community based* – there must be ownership of the ministry by the Christian community in any given area being served.

3. *Tangible* – the ministry must be something that North Americans can see, feel, and touch, and thus understand and be motivated to support.

Horizon is dedicated to raising up a new generation of Africans who are transformed from lives of desperation to becoming "a thousand suns over Africa," young men and women who have been saved, physically speaking, and awakened, spiritually speaking, to a grateful response to God's transforming and healing love. Horizon is to be a family for children without families, a divine agent that *models* the compassionate love of God that, unfortunately, some others preach more than live. The desired result, returning to Horizon's theme verse of Malachi 4:2, is that children by the thousands who had been imprisoned and likely doomed by poverty, disease, and hopelessness will be freed and "go out and leap like calves released from the stall"!

UNITY WITH ALL TRUE BELIEVERS

Horizon's North American officers and directors realized in 2008 that a formal statement of theological belief was needed. Various agencies, donors, congregations, foundations, and African ministry partners occasionally requested or even required public clarity in this regard. Deciding to provide such clarity, it was natural that the board of directors would turn to its secretary, Barry L. Callen, a Christian theologian and author, to draft such a statement for its consideration. As he proceeded to do this, he understood that the goal was to state strong Christian and mission convictions without building any unnecessary walls that would make Horizon appear denominational or divisive or bound to a given culture.

Callen created the requested theological draft, which was reviewed and accepted by the Horizon board of directors in its meeting of February 23, 2008. It reads:

Horizon International is a non-denominational Christian ministry motivated by this vision: *"But for you who revere my name, the sun of righteousness shall rise with healing in its wings.*

You shall go out leaping like calves from the stall!" (Malachi 4:2, NRSV). Accordingly, Horizon reveres the name and mission of Jesus Christ, shining today as the sun of righteousness, and is dedicated to creating a world of hope for AIDS orphans and the Christian leaders and care-givers who serve them and their extended families.

Underlying this reverence and dedication are certain affirmations of Christian faith. Horizon International affirms with joy:

- Its belief in the one eternal God, Creator and Lord of the world, eternally existing as Father, Son, and Holy Spirit, governing all things according to the graciousness of the divine purpose.

- Its belief in the divine inspiration of the Bible, Old and New Testaments, revelation that is dependable for guiding all aspects of Christian belief, life, and mission in the world.

- Its belief that there is only one Lord and Savior for humanity, Jesus Christ, the Son of God, born in Bethlehem, resurrected in Jerusalem, and ever-living through the person of the Holy Spirit.

- Its belief that Jesus Christ sends his redeemed people into the world as the Father sent him, to save sinners, to work for justice in human societies, to embody compassion, and to bring hope to the lost, oppressed, and diseased.

- Its belief in the power of the Holy Spirit to reveal the identity and purposes of the Christ, to bring new birth and spiritual maturity to fallen humanity, to indwell believers so that a godly life can be lived, and to gift faithful disciples for sacrificial service to the church and the world.

- Its belief in the spiritual unity of all true believers in Jesus Christ, thus encouraging Horizon to cooperate gladly with all who share this vision, also honor these beliefs, and choose to join hands with this ministry.

- Its belief that Jesus Christ will return one day, bringing divine judgment, vindicating the faithful, eliminating evil, and initiating life that is blessed and everlasting for those who belong to the eternal Christ and have served faithfully in his mission.

The stance of being a "non-denominational" Christian ministry has required particular diligence at several points, including relationships with the Church of God (Anderson) movement. Three of the four founding members of Horizon's board of directors were clergypersons credentialed by this movement, and the fourth was a layperson in one of its congregations. The president, Robert W. Pearson, had recently been a prominent leader in this movement's North American ministries. Even so, the non-denominational assertion has been made consciously and seriously. Not only is Horizon not an arm of the Church of God movement, but it intends not to function as a ministry competitor – for instance, with the movement's own child sponsorship program, *Children of Promise*. On the other hand, neither does Horizon refuse to work with the Church of God movement if and when such cooperation is mutually desired.

By 2007 invitations had come asking that Horizon partner with the national assemblies of the Church of God in Uganda and Zambia. In the September 8, 2007, meeting of the board of directors, president Pearson sought the board's wisdom. Should being a ministry of the whole body of Christ include special avoidance of the Church of God movement, even when elements of this body approach Horizon with ministry partnership proposals? The board discussed this question and made clear that being non-denominational does not mean approaching new ministry possibilities with fear or prior judgment. Relationships with the Church of God should not be sought, as they had not been, or necessarily rejected out of hand should they emerge. Horizon must remain open to whatever God seems to be directing. That means being open to the whole body of Christ and the full will of God.

Horizon's president said this in his January 9, 2002, report to the board of directors: "Horizon International exists to care for AIDS orphans in Africa. Our objective is to raise up, out of the tragedy of the AIDS pandemic, a new generation of African Christian leaders." As it does so, it must always be informed and inspired by the above beliefs. The God who first created is now full of love and compassion for the least of the creation, those little ones who suffer grief, hunger, disease, and helplessness. God calls faithful disciples, gifts them, and sends them on mission in the power and wisdom of the divine Spirit. Horizon is one means of channeling these divine gifts and expressing the Spirit's wisdom and power for the benefit of African children orphaned because of HIV/AIDS.

EVEN MY DOGS HAVE BEDS!

The ministry of Horizon International has been based on a vision of the dramatic human need in southern and eastern Africa, and on faith both that God has called for this need to be addressed and that God will provide whatever is necessary in relation to this call. If people who lack vision tend to perish, and those who have vision tend to accomplish great things, then Horizon's ministry has never been in danger of failure or managing only little accomplishments. There has been much vision!

Despite the constant presence of a guiding vision, one member of Horizon's founding board of directors, in fact the vice-president, admits readily to having begun his board service without this vision filling his being. Eric Dwiggins was a committed Christian, a good businessman, and certainly a willing servant, but he had significant questions and real hesitations about putting first in his own life a priority on AIDS orphans who lived so far away from his Indiana home. He was an honest and straightforward man with a prefer-ence for the practical. Then things dramatically changed for him.

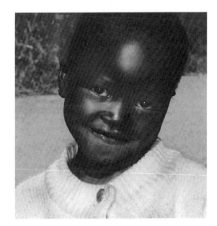

Tendai Machokoto

The big change came for Dwiggins when he received one of the routine mass mailings sent out by president Pearson to the Horizon donor and child-sponsor constituen-cies. It featured a photo of Tendai Machokoto, an African orphan girl who was about the same age as the Dwiggins' own daughter. This photo, randomly lying on his desk, soon began claiming the attention and reach-ing for the heart of Dwiggins. Through the photo, God was beginning to ask hard questions of this Horizon board member. Was Tendai really too far away to be helped? Was her need completely beyond this American's ability to address? Were her huge problems all self-inflicted? He had to admit that the answers were clearly "No!"

Then things began to happen quickly. In a meeting of Horizon's board of directors, Eric Dwiggins learned that there was an urgent need for bunk beds in Dawnview Park Children's Home in Harare, Zimbabwe. The Horizon kids living there were having to sleep on the hard floor – and Dwiggins was personally stunned by a thought that just grabbed him. The Dwiggins' two dogs both had nice beds! Once home, Eric asked his wife Tearle how much money was in their checkbook. There was enough extra to buy eleven bunk beds for orphans in Zimbabwe, so they did. Now a little of their money was on its way across the Atlantic Ocean – not too far away after all. Even so, Dwiggins had no intent of going himself. At least, that is what he thought. God was at work changing his life path.

Only months later, this Pendleton, Indiana, businessman and Horizon board member was traveling to Africa with Horizon's 2003 Vision Tour. Soon he found himself sitting in the Dawnview Park Children's Home on one of the very bunk beds that he and Tearle had purchased! But that was not all. Being very concerned about getting sick in that environment, he was washing his hands frequently, trying to avoid any excessive touching of the little children who may have AIDS themselves. While sitting, trying to stay clean and safe, a little girl landed on his lap. She was very sick with a high fever – just the thing he feared for himself! Even so, he forgot his caution and held her closely. It was none other than Tendai whose photo in an Horizon mailing had begun to grip Eric's heart and open him to Horizon's vision! His heart was broken. It was beginning to open wide with loving compassion.

As the ministry vision of Horizon began pouring into the heart of Eric Dwiggins, he began to think often of one Bible verse: "Since there will never cease to be some in need on the earth, I therefore command you, 'Open your hand to the poor and needy neighbor in your land'" (Deut. 15:11). There now was no more hesitation for this Christian man, and his earlier question had its answer. Could Horizon make a difference in the face of a pandemic troubling the earth? The answer is "Yes," one child at a time! For him, the first one was Tendai. God was calling, gifting, and sending. Eric Dwiggins and all Horizon leaders were anxious to hear and go.

Timothy Kumfer was now one of many who were ready, even determined to go on an African mission. He attended a major event of Promise Keepers in February, 2003, and was challenged to somehow embrace the pain and challenge of the African AIDS crisis. Jerry Grubbs, a fellow Church of God (Anderson) leader, helped him find a practical way to engage this fresh ministry call, directing him to Robert Pearson of Horizon International. Kumfer's people in Columbia City, Indiana, soon knew that something significant had happened to their pastor, and they began catching the vision with him. The children collected pennies to help their pastor get to Africa in July, 2003. He traveled with Pearson to Zimbabwe and South Africa.

They stayed in the Kingdom Hotel in Victoria Falls, Zimbabwe, a tourist center in this troubled country because of the impressive water falls on the Zambezi River. Kumfer encountered a luxurious setting featuring bountiful buffets for visitors. It was such a dramatic disconnect from the poverty and orphan crisis just beyond the hotel grounds. Pearson called the ironic circumstance "the Holocaust of our generation!" Kumfer determined that he would do something to help, and the something would be through Horizon's ministry. He had to be able to tell his children and grandchildren one day that he had seen what was happening and had done something about it!

Where, then, did Horizon International begin? The first answer should not be geographic. It actually began in the heart of God, and then as divine inspiration of a man. It began with the biblical story of the compassionate God now come in Jesus Christ. From that story came a call to generous openness to the neighbor, and especially to the orphan. It began in a transitional time in Robert Pearson's life, in a first trip to Africa, in a broken heart in the face of a pandemic, in a restaurant in Anderson, Indiana, as a small group of men gathered to forge some way forward.

Finally, there came a specific place of beginning. First, there was God in Israel and then in Jesus Christ; coming now was the great need in the country of South Africa, and the presence of God in that place. Soon

Horizon would be ministering in several countries of southern and eastern Africa. But first, the initial place of Horizon service would be a deeply troubled township near Capetown, South Africa.

A Place to Begin: Kayamandi

Where and with whom could an actual ministry beginning for Horizon be made in Africa? The problem was surely there, a devastating human crisis, especially in the countries of southern and eastern Africa. The divine call to this crisis had come to president Pearson and already had resulted in the beginnings of a new ministry organization, Horizon International, as a framework through which God's call could address the problem. A sturdy set of Christian beliefs, biblically based, was firmly in place to undergird the envisioned new enterprise. A gifted and committed board of directors had been recruited. Partners in Africa and a ministry strategy were already emerging. What was still needed were initial project locations and a widening circle of supporters in North America to make actual ministry possible.

In the face of the urgent need for supporters, president Pearson turned first to previous friends and colleagues. A few of these were Donald and Deborah Bergstrom, pastoring in Houston, Texas, Bob and Bonnie Powlison, active Christians in Aurora, Colorado, Bob and Lynetta Allenbrand in Portland, Oregon, and Larry and Joyce Hartman in California – who became Horizon's very first monthly donors.

Bob and Lynetta Allenbrand

Pearson had known the Bergstroms since 1993 when they had come to San Diego – Pearson was then area administrator for the Church of God (Anderson) in southern California. Word of Horizon's beginning

Donald and Deborah Bergstrom

was sent to Don Bergstrom, then pastoring in California. Soon moving to pastor in Houston, Texas, under Don's leadership the First Church of God there asked Pearson to speak at its Faith Promise convention in January, 2003. The next year a series of trips to Africa began the personal involvement of several people in this church. This involvement was greatly deepened by the concert appearance at First Church in May, 2005, of Horizon's Kuyasa Kids Choir (see chapter five). This was now a Horizon congregation! Such a process of congregational enlistment was repeated over and over.

In November, 2001, Robert Pearson called the Powlisons in Colorado. Over the phone, they heard the passionate voice of a man anxious to tell the story of Horizon's call from God and the great need of the children in Africa. This touched Bob and Bonnie and they became regular supporters immediately. They participated in Horizon's first Vision Tour to Africa in early 2003, and later Bonnie Powlison would become a member of the board of directors and then treasurer of Horizon International.

Bonnie and Robert Powlison

With numerous such people catching the Horizon vision and offering assistance, it finally was time to act on the ground in Africa. One ministry site was approved by Horizon's board of directors on January 9, 2002. It was a ministry already in motion, one involving HIV+ orphans in Masiphumelele, a black township of about 16,000 people adjacent to

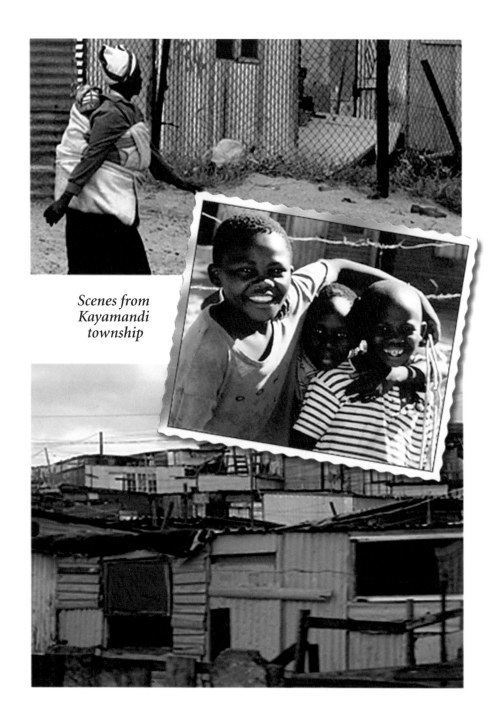

Scenes from Kayamandi township

the city of Fish Hoek on the Atlantic side of southernmost South Africa. The local Horizon partner would be John Thomas, pastor of King of Kings Baptist Church of Fish Hoek and a member of the AIDS Advisory Council of the South African government.

As it would turn out, however, this site would not be in Horizon's ministry future. Having quality ministry partners "on the ground" is crucial for effective ministry in Africa. John Thomas certainly would have been all of that. Even so, soon after the partnership was envisioned, Thomas traveled to Barcelona, Spain, to attend an HIV/AIDS conference. While there, he suffered a heart attack. Priorities had to change. Horizon suspended its emerging AIDS orphan ministry in Masiphumelele in order to focus its efforts elsewhere.

Approved in that same January 9, 2002, meeting by Horizon's board of directors was another ministry site, what would turn out to be the first actual one for Horizon. It was in Kayamandi, a Black township adjacent to the city of Stellenbosch in the Capetown, South Africa, area. The drama and tragedy of the townships in this area have roots in the 1920s when national law began forcing Black Africans and "Coloureds" to live in designated locations. The first, Langa township, was planned with wide streets, flood lights, and a police station at the single entry point to allow easy control of the inhabitants. Langa and other townships soon became shameful showplaces of apartheid. They featured human masses of misery, isolated as much as possible from the larger public. For instance, Khayalitsha was developed in the 1980s for 120,000 people. By 1990 its population had reached 450,000, with eighty percent unemployed and a very high HIV infection rate.

The Kayamandi township was chosen for Horizon's beginning because of its great need and the availability of local contacts who were prepared to assist. The local Horizon partners, in addition to Cassie and Jenny Carstens, would be a group of pastors from Kayamandi and Stellenbosch. Of the two mission strategies sometimes employed by North American ministries, home-based care and full-service orphanages, the first was envisioned for Kayamandi. With the help of the local pastors, the most needy children could be identified and placed in Christian homes, avoiding the sterile culture created by orphanages.

Horizon would seek to build a multi-purpose community center in this township to house a wide range of services to support the home-based orphan care. The sponsorship and care of each child would be funded by monthly gifts from compassionate North Americans.

Robert Pearson had met Cassie and Jenny Carstens on his first trip to Africa in August, 2001. Their ministries were centered in Stellenbosch, a university city near Capetown. On his second trip to Africa, Pearson had met many other people and visited the AIDS-related social services and Christian ministries already operating in the Stellenbosch area. The Carstens and he had convened area pastors to seek their guidance and assistance. They had pointed him to the great need in Kayamandi, noting how they might help if Horizon would come. Now, with the Carstens as new Horizon partners on the scene, these numerous contacts, and the offer of local pastoral support, the location for Horizon's beginning seemed obvious.

Nearly one in five South Africans call Xhosa their mother tongue. The name Kayamandi consists of *ikhaya* (home) and *imnandi* (sweet). But the reality is hardly that way. Kayamandi is a predominantly Black township that reflects the sad reality of South Africa's apartheid era. This ironically named "sweet home" is located on the outskirts of Stellenbosch, an old, sophisticated, mostly White university center. The township developed rapidly in the 1940s and 1950s to house Black migrant workers on the farms of the Stellenbosch area. It became a world where some 30,000 black Africans live in a virtual shack jungle, a squatter community with a poor infrastructure, to say the least. The unemployment rate of Kayamandi was about forty percent, and the rates of malnutrition and HIV infection were alarmingly high.

Horizon International was about to make a difference in Kayamandi township. The first Vision Tour group sent by Horizon visited there. One participant, Bonnie Powlison, remembers vividly an especially big day. It was March 3, 2003, dedication day for the Community Center that now had come into the possession of the local Horizon-related body, soon to be known as *Kuyasa Empowerment*. It had been substantially refurbished with a lot of hard physical labor. Unfortunately, water from the power washer had created a mud puddle at the entrance to the building, ruining

66

*Moments of
dedication formality
and fun*

Jenny Carstens speaks at the Community Center dedication

the hope of a dirt-free facility for the big event. It didn't matter. All the locals were used to difficult odds having to be overcome.

The mayor of the city of Stellenbosch, local pastors, and the principal of Kayamandi High School were all there for the big dedication. A catered meal was served on tables covered with cloths and flower centerpieces. All present were asked to write prayers on slips of paper and attach them to the wall beside a wooden cross, and to pour water into a ceremonial pitcher representing the overflowing prayers of the community. A dance group of local young people entertained. Horizon's coming was cause for celebration!

This day of dedication was an historic event that stretched well beyond Horizon's young ministry. It was a symbol of the launching of Horizon in the township; it also was the first time in the history of the area that representatives of the four South African people groups shared such a celebration together – Black, Brown, Dutch Africana, and English/British. Horizon was poised to serve orphans, yes, but it also was being a catalyst for weakening racial and cultural barriers that had long maintained hurtful practices of discrimination. To really care for orphans means more than clothing and feeding them; it means transforming the communities in which they must live. At least in a small way, such transformation had begun in Kayamandi.

In the years to come, Horizon would impact this Kayamandi township community in many significant ways. Thanks to funding from the Regis Foundation in 2007, Horizon's local organization partner, *Kuyasa Horizon Empowerment*, would be able to launch a new feeding program for the Kuyasa Center in Kayamandi. A nutritiously balanced meal would be provided daily to some two hundred hungry children during the after-school program. Horizon's Cindy Nixon, initially a ministry intern in Kayamandi, would later report that she was often asked by students in her classes for something to eat. "It is hard to focus and learn," she said with pain in her voice, "when the students are hungry and without hope of a meal." At least for the Horizon children, this painful circumstance would be ending!

Kayamandi township might have been the obvious place for Horizon to begin its African ministries, but managing to begin at all was a miracle for this new and largely unfunded ministry. In the face of a devastating pandemic, president Pearson gave his formal presidential report to the second meeting of Horizon's board of directors, convened on January 9, 2002, in Pendleton, Indiana. Covering the first months of Horizon's existence, ending December 31, 2001, there had been a total of $5,052 in disbursements. There was a fund balance of $827 and $900 in monthly support commitments. This was not much in the face of a world-scale human disaster, but it was a beginning. The president's salary, supplemented by his salary at the Pendleton church where he was pastoring, would be drawn only as it was actually raised – and, at first, not much of it was.

And what about those initial Horizon ministry partners in South Africa? How could salaries be paid abroad when the organization's president was barely being paid at home? It would have to be a matter of creativity, faith, and good fortune – probably better said to be divine provision. Cassie Carstens was about half-time with Horizon, with his salary underwritten by a group of South African businessmen. Jenny Carstens was full-time with Horizon, with half of her salary underwritten by a South African surgeon and the other half to be paid by Horizon in response to fresh fundraising efforts in the United States. This certainly was a faith venture, but one being inspired by God – thus there was hope that this ministry had a future despite its fragile beginning.

The fragile beginning of Horizon was tied intentionally to the fundamental beliefs of Horizon's founders and officers. These beliefs were biblically informed and judged to be Spirit directed. All Horizon leaders were committed Christians seeking to represent and work with the entire Christian community as agents of the compassionate Christ on behalf of desperate children. They also were prepared to sacrifice and innovate as necessary.

Here is one of many early examples of sacrifice. Michael and Diane Carey decided that they were willing to move from Casper, Wyoming, to Indiana in 2005. He became a volunteer financial planner and project manager for Horizon and she began coordinating a trans-Atlantic prayer ministry on behalf of Horizon and its difficult mission under God. Only serious prayer and self-sacrifice like this would be adequate for the

Diane and Michael Carey

challenge involved. God had called, and somehow God would provide.

As new field representatives for Horizon beginning in 2008, Win and Nancy Clark described as follows their response to God's call for them to join the Horizon team: "We are excited about being the hands and feet of Jesus!" A brochure of Horizon reports that 30 million of the world's 40 million people living with HIV/AIDS are in southern and eastern Africa.

Of these, 12 million are orphaned children fourteen years old and younger. What would be Horizon's response to this tragic situation?

That Horizon brochure projects an answer: "It is time for the Body of Christ to step up and lead the spiritual, social, and physical transformation of HIV/AIDS orphans!" Doug and Sandy Ehrgott were also now on board as Global Team Builders, bringing with them so much experience, enthusiasm, and a sense of divine calling.

Nancy and Win Clark

The Allenbrands, Bergstroms, Careys, Carstens, Clarks, Ehrgotts, Powlisons, and many others were now joining board of director members Callen, Dwiggins, Jenness, and Pearson by offering their hands and feet, their time and dollars, to the compassionate ministry of Jesus Christ.

Beyond influential and committed people, the events of one particular day in July, 2002, became a breakthrough. They were milestone happenings, holy hours graced by God. Looking back later, one could see that this special day was what really enabled Horizon to begin effective ministry in Kayamandi township in South Africa. Jenny Carstens, Cassie

Carstens, and Robert Pearson were guest speakers at St. Paul's Apostolic Church in Kayamandi. It was pastored by Baldwin Mantsai who was heading the new orphan-care screening committee recently formed to assist Horizon launch its local ministry with integrity.

It happened rather suddenly and unexpectedly during the worship service. A crowd of singing Christians from another local

Doug and Sandy Ehrgott

fellowship arrived and joined the gathering. It was an historic crossing of denominational boundaries happening only because of a common commitment to a larger cause – serving AIDS orphans in the community. A joint celebration dance began beautifully, symbolizing an unusual togetherness in the mission of Jesus Christ. Then the crowd, already enlarged, began to march out of St. Paul's and move through Kayamandi, going from church to church, singing praise songs in the local language, and gathering more and more people along the way.

This traveling festival of Christian joy was highlighting a critical fact. The local pastors, the gatekeepers of the community, were announcing the legitimacy of Horizon's new ministry among them. At the last church stop, a modest and now very crowded setting with dirt floor and tin roof, Cassie Carstens, a Dutch Reformed minister, made a very important statement to the assembly. His European-based church had been strongly identified with the earlier apartheid era in South Africa. Carstens was now saying what the locals had long waited to hear from a White man:

> *For years we forced you to serve us –*
> *now it's our turn to voluntarily serve you!*

This statement spread through Kayamandi like a healing wildfire. It was a new Pentecost experience. There were many tongues, yes, but only one mission experience under God. Horizon was solidly rooted in Scripture and now had its feet solidly planted on African soil. If the first Pentecost in Jerusalem had launched the church's worldwide mission,

*Robert Pearson, center foreground, leading a
"Pentecost parade" in Kayamandi township*

this Pentecost day in Kayamandi had launched Horizon's mission in
Africa, enlivened by the same sending and empowering Spirit of God.
Horizon had arrived to serve the needy children in the name and with
the love of God, and in partnership with the leaders of God's people in
that place.

Craig White

Chapter Four

BUILDING THE HOME BASE

The ministries of Horizon International were growing rapidly in South Africa. With Horizon's involvement in other nations likely to follow very soon, difficult questions were obvious. Where would all the needed money come from? Who would handle the growing mass of administrative details? How could increasing numbers of donors, partner organizations, child sponsors, and governments be kept properly informed and satisfied that the funding given was being handled responsibly?

An ever-expanding financial and administrative infrastructure would have to be built. A responsible ministry requires it. Committed staff persons would have to be found and funded. With God's help, ways would be found to get it all done. Faith just assumes that, when God calls, God provides. And God did!

Popularly known as Bono, Paul Hewson of the Irish rock band *U2* has championed the cause of HIV/AIDS, especially since 1999. He has received a Nobel Peace Prize nomination, an honorary knighthood by the United Kingdom, and the designation "Person of the Year" by *Time* magazine in 2005. Bono once was quoted as saying, "Whenever you see darkness, there is extraordinary opportunity for the light to burn brighter." He knew that the dense darkness caused by the HIV/AIDS pandemic is an engulfing midnight of blackness for millions of families, especially in southern Africa.

From a Christian perspective, this darkness can be viewed as a great opportunity for the church to let the light of Christ shine brightly. That is where Horizon International entered the scene. It has been driven by the troubling awareness of an enormous human need, and by an accompanying call from God to spread the compassionate light of Jesus Christ in this great darkness. The natural question always has been, "How?" How could a small, volunteer board of directors, an overworked president who at first was also pastoring a church, and a modest group of North American donors be effective in conveying the light of Christ in such an awful darkness?

By 2003 the president and board of directors of Horizon were about the task. They were busy building the new organization, troubleshooting its earliest efforts, and responding as possible to an accelerating array of ministry opportunities and challenges. This was being done with virtually no staff in the home office and a president whose considerable energy and creativity were being stretched to their limits. Conversation among members of the board of directors sometimes turned to a serious caution.

The analogy occasionally voiced in board meetings was of a wall growing higher and higher, but without a sturdy foundation under it. Such, it was said, is not a wall, but a foolhardy structure waiting for its time of certain collapse. The point was clear. How could Horizon avoid being a disaster waiting to happen? Expansion had to be measured with care, matched with available resources and support structures, and handled responsibly. Too much too fast could be a formula for failure.

Here was the persistent question for Horizon board members and officers. How could so many opportunities be grasped (the higher and higher walls of a wonderful structure) and, at the same time, there be put in place an adequate base of support staff, infrastructure, and especially income streams sufficient to hold it all in place? Board members agreed that the foundation of Horizon's ministry must be strengthened and its integrity protected. Promises must not be made that could not be fulfilled. Projects must not be started that could not be completed. Warned one board member, "We must not allow ourselves to become a mile wide and only an inch deep!" There was no disagreement, only the constant search for ways to be all that God appeared to be wanting Horizon to be.

DEVELOPING AN ADEQUATE BASE

A letter dated May 23, 2003, represents an important milestone for Horizon International. It was from the Internal Revenue Service of the United States and announced that Horizon had been approved as a Christian humanitarian 501c3 not-for-profit organization. This formal recognition brought new rules to be followed and significant reporting obligations to be met; it also meant that all contributions to the ministry would be exempt from federal income tax, retroactive to the earliest donors. This benefit was necessary for building the financial base of the young ministry.

Horizon's attorney, Wes Schrock, had assisted with this IRS filing. Its success had been helped by president Robert Pearson having been very careful about following responsible rules related to financial dealings, and by the corporate secretary, Barry Callen, having kept thorough minutes of all meetings of the board of directors from the beginning. In addition, the board had always been kept fully informed and had taken specific actions to approve all ministry projects in Africa calling for any financial obligations on Horizon's part. Appropriate records had been kept despite the lack of staff or computer support that made such work so burdensome.

It had been vital for Horizon that its president, beyond being passionate about the ministry, was a detail person and a natural networker of people. In addition, Robert Pearson's effective public speaking was essential for the early building of the ministry's financial base and fund of goodwill. The last four months of 2002 serve as an example of his tireless activity. He spoke at a Horizon banquet in Kansas City, preached on various occasions around southern California, addressed the crowd during the intermission of a benefit concert for Horizon in Indiana, then at a Horizon banquet in Denver, and finally preached at three different churches in southern Florida. One was the Kendall Church of God in Miami that had given about $3,000 to help launch Horizon. Such a schedule, while exhausting, had not been optional.

Special offerings were taken at these banquet events and in these churches. Sometimes Horizon was then placed in a congregation's mission budget and the people encouraged by their pastor to consider individual sponsorships of children in Africa. An example was pastor John Morden in Elkhart, Kansas.

Samantha Morden (Frazier)

Morden had been receiving regular Horizon mailings, but had given this new ministry little thought until he got a call from president Pearson. He was impressed by Pearson's enthusiasm for this ministry and his great compassion for the orphans so far away. An invitation was extended for Pearson to come to Kansas in June, 2004, to share his vision with the congregation and its mission team. The result? It was more than anyone would have expected.

Horizon went into that church's mission budget, Tammi Evans became Horizon's first summer intern in South Africa in 2004, and a year later Morden's niece, Samantha Morden (Frazier), was referred to Horizon and soon became a major staff person in the ministry's home offices in Pendleton, Indiana. In 2005 pastor Morden moved to the South Side Church of God in St. Louis, Missouri, taking with him a commitment to Horizon. Soon Horizon was also in that congregation's budget.

Tammi Evans

Such personal contacts by Robert Pearson and the other forms of Horizon's communication led to more and more commitments to the new ministry. The resulting income stream grew, and it was handled with care despite the lack of staff and computerized accounting infrastructure. The stream was tracked partly by the services of accountant Randy Wilson, the watchful eye of a detail-oriented president, and the financial expertise and business experience of Jeffrey Jenness and Eric Dwiggins, members of the board of directors. Wilson was president of Integrated Tax Services of Pendleton, Indiana, and a member of the North Anderson Church of God. He would assist further by identifying much-needed financial software.

A monthly donor newsletter was soon going out from the president to a mailing list of 150. A packet of materials for interested congregations was developed, with at least a dozen churches considering regular support of Horizon. Proposals for targeted support were before a foundation (United States) and the Hannalie Ruppert Trust (South Africa). Three regional Horizon rallies were planned on different parts of the west coast of the United States for the spring of 2003, two in California and one in Portland, Oregon. Many seeds were being planted; some of them were already beginning to bear fruit.

Where did Horizon's finances stand after its first full year of operation? Donors had contributed approximately $90,000 in 2002. That number increased substantially to $226,400 in 2003, with the approved operational budget for 2004 rising sharply to $542,333. That was only the beginning. Total revenue for Horizon in 2006 was $943,717, with this number expanding upward to $1,432,924 in 2007, and with the 2009 budget expanding further to an amazing $2,540,460. Such dramatic growth, while gratifying, only heightened the need for aggressive fundraising – some elements of the budget still would be spent only if actually raised. It also increased the need to maintain detailed and accurate balance sheets and statements of profit and loss, and to be conscious of the best in accounting practices, with all their legal ramifications and required reports.

This ministry soon was large enough that it no longer was flying "under the radar" of various regulatory agencies in the United States. A growing number of financial reports was necessary for Horizon's internal use and for the information of potential large donors, foundations, state registrations, and filings with the U. S. Internal Revenue Service. Accordingly, Horizon initially retained Gasparovic Tax Services of Pendleton, Indiana, to prepare employee W-2s and 1099s, do filings with the IRS and the Indiana Department of Revenue, and maintain the needed financial statements for regular review by the president and board of directors. George and Norma Gasparovic, local Christian and civic leaders, had developed a passion for Horizon's new ministry and were glad to have their firm assist.

Horizon funded a 2006 financial audit of *Horizon Thusanang*, a ministry partner in Limpopo Province, South Africa. This was judged necessary to maintain full public integrity of that organization's operation. That was in Africa. Back in the United States, the Horizon board of directors determined in September, 2007, that Horizon International should seek for itself the earliest possible certification by the respected organization Evangelical Christian Financial Accountability (ECFA). The board directed that in 2008 an independent audit of Horizon's 2007 books be conducted (in part to qualify for ECFA certification). While costly, this audit was hardly optional. The ministry also began the complex process of registering Horizon in all states where it is required. Among other things, this registration would protect Horizon from challenges by potential donors who might claim to have been solicited for gifts without having given advance permission to do so.

Horizon began receiving guidance from two financial consultants, Howard Taylor of the Rediger Taylor Group and Robert Norvell of A. G. Edwards. A professional audit of Horizon's entire operation for 2007 was conducted in 2008 by Yount and Company, L.L.C., of Indianapolis, Indiana, at a cost of $7,500. The result was affirming for Horizon's board of directors and staff, and it was reassuring for the many donors to the ministry. This audit also pointed to a series of growth needs in various financial practices – typical challenges faced by young not-for-profit organizations. Horizon had operated with full integrity and handled well a mass of detail, and it had done so with limited staff and limited computer infrastructure.

Staff member Marena Gammons had been registering Horizon in the states not requiring a copy of an outside audit. Now that the audit was complete, she would begin registration in the other states, with the goal of Horizon being formally recognized in all fifty by the end of 2009. Also in 2009, Horizon contracted with the company E-Tapestry to receive greatly enhanced accounting and reporting services. While costly to contract, such services promised to bring efficiency and cost savings to the financial operation. The increasing flow of dollars was finally being matched by an increasing ability to handle, track, and report them with clarity and confidence.

A GROWING LEADERSHIP TEAM

Building an adequate financial base for a rapidly expanding ministry would require development of a competent staff in the home offices in the United States. It also would require more than a part-time president. Robert Pearson explained to Horizon's board of directors in January, 2004, that he was considering resigning his pastoral role at the Pendleton, Indiana, congregation, noting that the church deserved more than he now was able to give. Further, Horizon had grown at an exponential rate and would grow further only if it were given increased attention.

The office of the president was central to fulfilling the need for growing attention to many of Horizon's administrative, fundraising, and group-travel tasks. But he was only part-time with Horizon since he was still pastoring the Pendleton congregation. The congregation's associate pastor, Todd Faulkner, was about to graduate from Anderson University's School of Theology and, it appeared to Robert Pearson, would be a competent replacement for the senior role at the church. Horizon's board of directors judged that a full-time president would be highly desirable, despite the reality that funding a move to full-time would be an act of faith. Pearson proceeded to end his tenure with the church, willing to launch out on faith. The board was pleased and fully supportive.

Horizon's continuing expansion, however, required more than a full-time president. It required a board of directors comprised of more than the four men who had functioned in this central role from the beginning. One of the four, Jeffrey Jenness, had to resign from the board in 2005 because of the increasing responsibilities of his own professional roles – although he would remain a great friend and consultant for Horizon. While the bylaws of the corporation called for "at least three" board members, now envisioned was a move from four to seven.

Considerable attention was given to the most desirable categories of potential persons to serve on the board. The hope, in part, was to highlight the inter-denominational nature of Horizon. Since the original four members were all men associated with the Church of God (Anderson), women and persons affiliated with other Christian communions were desired. Naturally, if possible, new members should bring with them significant financial resources or good connections to others with such resources. Strong Christian commitment, unusual wisdom, and a real heart for a mission to children in Africa would be required of any candidate. The number of board members increased from four to six in 2005 and then to seven in 2006. Three of these seven were now women.

Bonnie Powlison

Bonnie Powlison (later to become Horizon's treasurer) was serving on the management team for Epson America, living in Aurora, Colorado, attending Creekside Church, and had participated in Horizon's first Vision Tour in southern Africa in 2003. She and her husband Robert were "overwhelmed" by the need that Horizon was addressing and excited about what "our small contribution could accomplish with God's multiplication applied."

Mary Beth Jackson had been with the 2001 group in South Africa that gave Robert Pearson his first exposure to the need that Horizon was then created to address. She later reported that she was "overwhelmed by the expertise and commitment of Horizon's board members," and she was glad to be on the growing edge of a young mission organization. Having traveled back to Africa and met many of Horizon's local leaders, she was further impressed with "the fantastic people" that Horizon had recruited, and she appreciated the fact that Pearson himself was "a strong leader who remains teachable."

Lisa Scaling

Lisa Scaling had taught business at Casper College in Casper, Wyoming, and was a corporate leader of Christian Solidarity Worldwide, an organization serving persecuted Christians. A great day for her was October 30, 2005, at Highland Park Community Church. Her son was being baptized and Robert Pearson spoke to the congregation about Horizon. The next summer, Scaling and her son were in South Africa with Horizon. Soon, she reports, "the desire to get involved in this incredible ministry was tugging at my heart." She would travel again to Africa in 2007, be a Horizon child sponsor, assist with the concert tour of the Kuyasa Kids coming to Casper (see chapter five), and become a member of the Horizon board of directors.

Christopher Dancy

Christopher Dancy was the fourth new board member. He is a retired management professional with Herman Miller, Inc. He lives near Sacramento, California, and serves as a lay leader of the Antelope Road Christian Fellowship. In June, 2006, he first brought his considerable energy, business expertise, and deep Christian commitment to Horizon's board of directors. His daughter Trysha became an Horizon intern, in part the reason that her father went to South Africa in 2008 and assisted president Pearson with the emergency arrangements for getting food into the troubled country of Zimbabwe (see chapter six).

In January, 2009, Dancy took the lead in developing Horizon's first employee handbook, traveling from California to Indiana to help introduce and explain it to the Horizon staff. He had just hosted a retreat meeting of the Horizon board of directors in California where final touches had been put on this handbook. Visiting the Antelope Road Christian Fellowship in Citrus Heights during this meeting, the board members celebrated with the people the several ways that this local fellowship had assisted Horizon's ministry from nearly its beginning. The pastor, Rhodes Pringle, and his wife Jolene are considered highly valued members of the Horizon "family."

As the board of directors thought about its own ideal membership and expanded its numbers, it also recognized the potential legal liability related to the volunteer service of its members. The board was leading work so closely with children in multiple cultures, countries, and legal systems. The issue of the potential bonding of Horizon's directors and officers became an occasional item for discussion. Such insurance proved

Antelope Road Christian Fellowship mission leaders.
Rev. Rhodes Pringle pictured far left

very expensive, virtually prohibitive for the young ministry organization. Positive factors that moderated the risk included Indiana law being favorable to leaders of not-for-profit corporations (apart from fraud or criminal neglect) and Horizon's approach of forming grassroots organizations, local Horizon-related bodies established legally in Africa.

The board of directors, having researched this situation, was committed to the ministry task and willing to proceed without formal bonding. The legal risk, however, existed, and maybe even more so from increasing numbers of persons traveling to Africa through Horizon as members of vision tours and work camps, and a few as ministry interns. Steps were taken to formalize carefully worded documents of waiver that all such persons would have to sign in advance of travel. To date, there had been no problem, but the ministry had to be protected from the future possibility.

All of these developments were natural for a rapidly expanding ministry organization. With them came the need for enhanced communication with multiplying constituencies, including the development of a new web site to enable Horizon to reach the wider world through the internet. Todd Callen, son of Horizon board member Barry Callen, provided early ideas and encouragement. Sean Sheridan did the bulk of the work on the actual site development. The result was an important new means of sharing information and gathering new support. The web site address is *www.horizoninternationalinc.com.*

The many new administrative tasks were burdening the tiny Horizon staff in its Pendleton, Indiana, offices. At first, the president did much of the administrative work himself. Soon he was assisted by Sandy Alford as office administrator, and then also by Joyce Chapple who was the first person to serve as Coordinator for Child Sponsorships.

Others joined the staff over the years to address particular needs. One person of special importance, Samantha (Morden) Frazier, was a participant in Horizon's fall 2004 Vision Tour to Africa. She had spent part of her teenage years on mission with her parents in Kenya, East Africa. She now had arrived back in Africa with Horizon and soon was extremely impressed by the high levels of skill and commitment she saw in Horizon's team partners in South Africa and Zimbabwe. She was ready to become involved herself.

A graduate of Seattle Pacific University, Samantha had an uncle, John Morden, a Church of God pastor who had been very supportive of Horizon from almost its beginning. He had alerted "Sam" to this ministry and encouraged her involvement. Having then been on the Vision Tour in 2004, she was willing to move to Indiana and serve Horizon in any way she could. Soon a way was found to add her to the staff as an administrative assistant and supervisor of the *Out of Africa Gift Shop* recently opened in Pendleton, Indiana (see below). She was invited to the May 24, 2005, meeting of Horizon's board of directors to share the story of God's call on her life. It was a moving report. In the years to

Out of Africa Gift Shop

follow, she would emerge as a skilled, trusted, and long-term administrative leader, including becoming the manager of Horizon's home offices.

A welcome staff volunteer who came later from Casper, Wyoming, was Mary Rickart. She served in the home offices of Horizon from 2008 until 2009, returning then to her home to continue serving Horizon online and occasionally with tours of the Kuyasa Kids in the United States. She was replaced in December, 2009, by a full-time Administrative Assistant, Lynda Malysa. Together, then, Samantha Morden Frazier, Gayla Morgan, Lynda Malysa, and others formed a skilled and committed team serving Horizon daily in the organization's home offices.

Mary Rickart

Lynda Malysa

Beyond a full-time president and an increased number of board and staff members, some other expansion opportunities had come along by mere chance (understood by faith, of course, as divine providence). For instance, Robert Pearson was riding the Washington Metro Rail as part of his attending the "Prescription for Hope" international conference on HIV/AIDS in February, 2002. He found himself talking to a Steve Walker, deacon of a large Baptist church in North Carolina. They discovered that they had a common relation to the growing ministry in Masiphumelele, South Africa, and pastor John Thomas there. Assistance from this east coast congregation might now be available to Horizon. Neither Pearson nor Walker, however, could know of the coming heart attack of Thomas that would change Horizon's plans for an initial ministry launch in South Africa.

Many donors were giving regularly through Horizon by the end of 2004. Project giving was strong that year, totaling nearly $100,000 either in hand or promised and soon to be received. The monthly child sponsorships, at the very heart of Horizon's mission, were in addition. Special people with generous hearts were becoming part of the Horizon family. One was Bill Freije. Having met Mr. Freije in 2000 while networking in the Indianapolis area with Christian executives, Pearson called him after returning from his trip to Africa, telling him of the impact of the experience and of his new sense of calling to a ministry to orphans.

Bill Freije

Meanwhile, Bill, himself an industrial visionary and entrepreneur, had started Freije Water Treatment Systems in Indiana. Now hearing Pearson's story and divine calling, he felt moved by God to become personally involved. He says, "I saw the power and faithfulness of God at work in Bob. I found participation with Horizon so faith-building for myself." His commitment was that he would support Horizon in direct proportion to the growth of his company. God has greatly blessed Freije and his company since then, and, in turn, Freije has been faithful to bless the children of Africa through Horizon. Currently, he sponsors fourteen African children, occasionally supports special projects, and reports this: "I smile when I think of Horizon." Bill Freije represents many others who have caught the vision and supported the ministry as they have been able.

CHILD SPONSORS

President Robert W. Pearson reported the following to Horizon International's board of directors on January 9, 2002: "We are not yet ready to launch a drive to solicit child sponsorship support, although several current donors have expressed interest. I project late spring or summer." Given its mission, and despite its organizational life still in the formative stage, the sponsorship of children was one of Horizon's first program priorities.

By the summer of 2002, the per-month cost of a child sponsorship had been set, along with the determination to keep administrative costs as modest as possible. Dollars received must yield maximum benefit for the children themselves. On August 27, 2002, with the screening assistance of Christian pastors in Kayamandi township and Stellenbosch near Capetown, South Africa, the first eight orphans were approved for sponsorship and matched with generous North Americans. The heart of Horizon's ministry had begun beating in earnest.

As effective sponsorship program must do more than get resources directly to the children. It also must plan for the regular linking of the children and their sponsors. Information must flow back and forth for the building of personal relationships. This was detailed work that Horizon's president could hardly do. It was time for securing a staff person, despite the lack of funds to support one.

Joyce Chapple stepped into this large gap. The owner/director of a daycare for young children near Horizon's home offices in Pendleton, Indiana, Chapple went to Africa with Horizon in March, 2003. Soon she was calling the trip "the best time in my life!" She recalled first landing in Zimbabwe, already late for a church service. The Horizon group changed clothes in an airport bathroom and hurried to the patiently waiting people. "I will never forget the welcome and honor they bestowed on us. Children, hugs, and

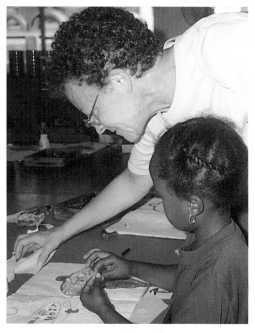

Joyce Chapple

88

smiles were everywhere! The children wanted to touch my skin and hair, likely never having been close to a white person before. I was honored and humbled."

Chapple recognized that Robert Pearson felt overwhelmed by the many opportunities and challenges that opened to Horizon during this eventful 2003 Vision Tour. She offered him her service because she wanted to help any way she could with "Africa's most innocent victims." Chapple was now in love with these precious children. Her offer was accepted gladly. There were only about fifty children being sponsored at first. The new coordinator agreed to work without salary until one hundred children had been sponsored – that number would enable Horizon to provide compensation for the sponsorship coordinator from the monthly administrative fee drawn from each sponsorship. A milestone day was certainly the one when Horizon had its first paid employee in North America, Joyce Chapple. Payment meant that the first one hundred children were under full sponsorship.

In January, 2005, the monthly support amount for a child was raised from $30 to $35 because the economic circumstances in Africa were severely limiting Horizon's ability to serve the needs of its children adequately. Then, in January, 2007, Joyce Chapple concluded her service with Horizon, having overseen the number of child sponsorships grow from about fifty to over eight hundred! She entered a Hospice ministry and needed to be free to travel with her husband and his work. She had made a major contribution to the early stages of Horizon's ministry.

By April, 2007, Gayla Morgan had assumed the crucial role of coordinating the child sponsorship program. She had taken early retirement from her General Motors career in Anderson, Indiana, and begun teaching business administration part-time and volunteering with the Red Cross. But one Sunday at Bethany Christian Church in Anderson she encountered Diane Carey who was sharing her great love of Horizon's work in Africa. Morgan had never heard of Horizon, although it was headquartered just a few miles from her home.

The two women met and soon Morgan was volunteering with Horizon. When Chapple retired, Carey urged Morgan to apply for the position. She did and assumed the role that soon would change her life and

Gayla Morgan

give her heart a new passion. This is "a ministry for me, not a job," she later reported, with a deep sense of being truly blessed. Horizon and the children of Africa were fortunate to have her skills and dedication on their side.

By 2008, Gayla Morgan had read many letters from child sponsors to their African children, and from the sponsored orphans back to their sponsors. Sometimes she would just cry – "These children are amazing. Some of their stories just break your heart." Morgan soon had the privilege of traveling around the United States three times with the Kuyasa Kids choir from South Africa (see chapter five). She says that "knowing what these kids have had to endure in their short lives, I'm amazed by them. They have virtually nothing, and yet they are happier than most of the kids in our American culture. They have such sweet spirits, are so grateful, and their faith is so strong!"

Morgan had brought with her to Horizon a rich background in sales and marketing, and a masters degree in management. In a September, 2007, meeting, the board of directors was pleased to receive a report from her of the number of African children then under Horizon's full sponsorship. The number had surpassed the one thousand mark and was growing weekly. The board was delighted both with the number, and with the quality attention that the coordinator was giving to the program's numerous details. By then, these children were distributed among four areas of South Africa, three areas of Zimbabwe, two areas of Uganda, and one area of Zambia.

TOTALS OF AFRICAN CHILD SPONSORSHIPS
As of November 1, 2009

Horizon International's African Centers	Number of Sponsored Children
South Africa	
KwaZulu – Natal – Izulu Orphan Project In three different villages	12
KwaZulu – Natal – MusaweNkosi Ministry In three different villages	14
Limpopo Province In twenty-four different villages	455
Western Cape Four different townships	263
Uganda	
Fort Portal	204
Jinga (Our Own Home Ministry)	30
Zambia	
Chongwe District and Lusaka-Chaisa Compound	125
Zimbabwe	
Bulawayo	67
Harare	360
Victoria Falls	19
Total of Sponsored Children in All Centers:	**1,549**

These children were reporting through regular letters to their U. S. sponsors. They were saying things like: "I don't feel like an orphan anymore!" and "My friends at school don't make fun of me anymore because I have a uniform like the rest of them, thanks to Horizon!" Here are lines from other letters from rescued children in South Africa and Zimbabwe. They represent so many more. The spelling and grammar are not perfect, but the feelings and love are so genuine.

I right this card to my wonderful people wishing you a marry Cristmas and good long life. You guys never give up on me ever since I lost so many people's in my life.

I am thanking you for the money you gave me because I've got food and clothes to wear. I am also going to the doctor when I am sick.

I would like to thank you so much for choosing to sponsor me. I really appreciate what you have done. May you always be blessed and may you be given more than you spend for me. I love you.

Your help really inspires me to dream big in life. Maybe one day I can make a difference in somebody's life.

Gayla Morgan was privileged to go to Africa herself in October, 2008, to attend Horizon's African Team Retreat convening in Lusaka, Zambia. She was so excited by this opportunity, getting to actually see the fruit of all the daily labor behind the scenes in the Pendleton, Indiana, offices. There now were so many children being sponsored through Horizon in so many places. Morgan became aware of a joy beyond the ability of mere words to describe. It was being experienced again and again. A child sponsor in North America would have the rare opportunity of actually meeting in person the African child being sponsored. The moment of meeting was always a burst of excitement, tense, a little awkward, and then just joy. Here are four examples.

1. **Patty Goffner**, member of an African-American Methodist congregation in Indianapolis, Indiana, read in an Indianapolis newspaper about Horizon's gift shop located in nearby Pendleton. She called Robert Pearson and then came to visit, not knowing that she and he shared a particular

church tradition. He helped her trace a relative of hers who had been a church leader in Jamaica. Goffner embraced the ministry vision of Horizon and soon became a child sponsor. She, Joyce Chapple, and Robert Pearson then traveled together to Africa in 2004. The experience was life-changing for her.

Goffner's African experience was all on the positive side. She carried with her to Africa a deep sadness.

Patty Goffner and Catherine

She had lost a granddaughter in a drive-by shooting in Indianapolis and now was sponsoring an African teenager about the same age. Goffner and her African "daughter" in Limpopo Province, South Africa, finally managed to meet in person – and a very emotional experience it was! Once back in the United States, Goffner told the University United Methodist Church in Indianapolis, "Meeting Catherine was one of the greatest thrills of my life!" One could only imagine Catherine's feelings.

Something Goffner probably didn't report to her church family was that, while visiting in Victoria Falls, Zimbabwe, Robert Pearson had shared an elephant ride and almost fell off – which could have been an inglorious ending to a brief Horizon presidency! Fortunately, he had managed to hold on.

2. **Dorinda Jacobson** of Casper, Wyoming, also went on a Horizon trip, telling her sponsored African girl in advance that she was coming to see her. Unfortunately, the girl misunderstood which group she would be in. The young African waited patiently and excitedly for this amazingly loving American visitor, but was devastated because Jacobson didn't arrive with the group! The girl dropped out of school for two weeks, experiencing depression at the loss of the most important relationship in her life.

Dorinda Jacobson's African daughter

When the reason for her depression was finally discovered, she was told about the mix-up, and soon the real reunion of a seventeen-year-old with her Horizon "mother" did happen. The girl had not been abandoned after all! Words cannot explain the rush of feelings that accompany the first meeting of an American mother and her African daughter.

3. **Jan and Barry Callen** from Anderson, Indiana had sponsored a young man in Limpopo Province, South Africa, for three years, occasionally

exchanging a letter or photo. But in 2007 they were on a Horizon Vision Tour and made arrangements to meet Leave (Liffy) Makgopa in person. Suddenly, there he and his grandmother were, standing beside the road just as planned – he speaks little English and was noticeably nervous.

Jan and Barry Callen with Liffy

The mini-bus stopped and out came the Callens with a camera, hugs, and a new backpack filled with school supplies for their "son." At first he was overwhelmed and hardly believed that the gifts were really for him to keep. But they were, as was the love of his North American "parents." The meeting lasted only thirty minutes, but the feelings and memories would last a lifetime. He explains in letters that his hope is to be a policeman. Many people around him need protection and justice, he says. With the help of Jesus, and knowing that two Horizon people from America love and will care for him, he will do his best.

4. **Jo and Morris Walter** of Fortville, Indiana, have sponsored Thabang Moshebela since 2005. He also lives in Limpopo Province, South Africa. They have been blessed to meet him twice as they traveled with Horizon groups. Here is their testimony: "We played, laughed, cried, prayed, and rejoiced with the children. We met missionaries who truly are living examples of God's outstretched hands and feet. Our treasures

Morris and Jo Walter with Thabang Moshebela

are more than the trinkets we found at the markets. They are in the smiles, the eyes, the hugs, the love, and the trust given through children and adults who are examples of the joy that comes when one lives for Christ, and daily believes that God is in control. We now see that we need Africa as much as Africa needs us. Our lives are forever changed!" With people like that on Thabang's side, a better future is really possible.

These occasional bursts of emotion and love between sponsor and child are made possible by the constant discipline of detailed administrative work behind the scenes, both in Horizon's home offices in North America and by its numerous administrators and caregivers on the ground in Africa. The child-sponsorship program requires the management of the flow of funds given and communication desired. Contact between each American sponsor and the African orphan builds acquaintance and commitment. Horizon must be sure that candidates for sponsorship are properly screened, and then it must supervise diligently the care actually delivered. There must be certainty that the funds sent for child support are spent properly and efficiently.

There is yet another need requiring wise and prompt management of the child sponsorship program. Difficult circumstances are created when committed sponsorship funds are not actually received from donors, for whatever reason. Sometimes a child needs to be re-sponsored. Sometimes emergency coverage of an unpaid account must happen so that the care of a child is not interrupted. Making this possible requires intentional planning.

This needed coverage caused by delinquent dollars was recognized early by Horizon's president and board of directors, and it was addressed by the establishment in 2003 of the Children's Reserve Fund. Sponsors were encouraged to give a little extra each month beyond the usual sponsorship amount. The excess money would go into this fund to ensure that no child would experience the interruption of support because of the failure of a donor to keep current with a financial commitment. Delinquent sponsorship accounts must be handled wisely and promptly or the human results on the ground in Africa are heartbreaking. In 2007, Marena Gammons from the Northview Christian Life Church in Carmel, Indiana, was added to Horizon's home staff as an administrative assistant to handle this and related tasks. The volunteer service of board member Eric Dwiggins has worked on occasion in an attempt to "close the back door" on delinquent accounts.

The administrative problem of handling child-sponsorship finances worsened further as the world experienced a major economic downturn in 2008. The United States was particularly hard hit. This forced some Horizon sponsors to make the hard priority decision to end their regular giving to an African child. Horizon personnel went into action to deal with this urgent problem. Bonnie Powlison, member of the board of directors, spread the word at her home church in Colorado, with the result that eight children were newly sponsored. Horizon donor Bill Freije turned to his own Indiana company and managed to get ten more children sponsored. Additional action would be needed since the depth and length of the economic downturn was yet unknown, and the needs of the children were as great as ever.

The board of directors responded by establishing a new strategy for handling sponsorship losses. It involved the painful plan of terminating particular children in given sets of circumstances. Such was judged necessary to ensure the solvency of the program as a whole and the uninterrupted support of those children most in need. It was an emergency move to be in effect only until the Children's Reserve Fund could be replenished and economic circumstances improved.

Meanwhile, Gayla Morgan had developed a new handbook on child sponsor policies and procedures to sharpen all aspects of the program's administration – in both the United States and Africa. She had opportunity to share this handbook with Horizon's African team partners during her trip to

Zambia in 2008. Thanks went out to all who were standing firm in trying times for the United States and, thus, for Horizon International. God, through his people, remained strong and fully committed.

A given child, of course, is not sponsored for life. Once high school graduation is accomplished, Horizon sponsorship usually ends. The ministry's concern, however, continues for the future well being of that grown-up child. One way to address this concern was an action taken by the board of directors in 2008. It established a two-tier child sponsorship program, one for the monthly sponsorship of a child's present needs (the original and standard program) and another at a higher monthly fee to enable the accumulation of money for the child's future educational needs beyond high school graduation and basic Horizon sponsorship. Sponsors are now encouraged to consider the higher tier for their children.

Caring for HIV/AIDS orphans had been the launching purpose of Horizon International. Across the first decade of the ministry's life, however, a wide range of support service activities evolved in several African countries. Even so, the orphan care ministry would remain central, with the other activities justified because they contribute in distinctive ways to the effective care of orphans. One support activity, this one in the United States, was an African gift shop. Another was the challenge of locating facilities that were affordable and adequate to serve Horizon's growing staff and administrative activities in its home offices.

AFRICAN GIFT SHOP AND HOME OFFICES

The first priority of Horizon International always has been to care for the immediate needs of the many children being sponsored in Africa. Once properly cared for by Horizon, the next priority has been to find ways to make these growing children productive individuals who could sustain themselves when adulthood came – and even become local or national leaders in their countries. African adults surrounding the sponsored orphans often needed employment so that they could survive themselves and then be freed to assist with orphan care. Constant creativity always has been required in order to find ways to meet such demanding priorities in what often have been very deprived and sometimes dangerous sets of circumstances.

Ways have been found. In Kayamandi, South Africa, and elsewhere, sewing machines were purchased by Horizon donors and soon people were making clothes for the children and uniforms for local schools. Some of what was produced could gain a profitable market if brought back to the United States and sold. As president Robert Pearson traveled in Africa, he began purchasing items in quantity and carrying or shipping them home. He and the board of directors dreamed of a way to market these items, partly to assist the African producers and partly to give a tangible public face to Horizon in central Indiana.

In October, 2003, Horizon staged the grand opening of the *Out of Africa Gift Shop* in the Pendleton Falls Park Plaza just opposite the congregation pastored by Robert Pearson. With Sandy Alford as manager and a volunteer staff, and with the generosity of Charles Clevenger, owner of the property, the first

Jenny Carstens instructs a sewing class

year's proceeds exceeded $7,000. Clevenger is a pharmacist by profession and, with his wife Kelly, own numerous commercial properties in and around Pendleton. Building their own home next to Pearson's rural Pendleton home was how they first became acquainted with Horizon.

Reports Charles Clevenger: "The Lord has blessed us in our work and Bob shared with us about the exciting ministry he had begun. I know that the Bible emphasizes the needs of orphans and widows, so I told Bob we'd like to help. We heard him preach and knew that God was using him. So we adopted our first Horizon child in 2002, in fact, we were one of the very first child sponsors. Then we learned that he needed a place to open an

Kelly and Charles Clevenger

African gift shop and we had a place available. We even loaned him a vehicle so that he could transport the initial shop inventory."

The profits from the gift shop's operation were used for start-up costs and the purchase of new inventory from Africa. Public visibility for the shop soon was gained by stories in local newspapers. President Pearson was interviewed on an African-American radio show, and a Horizon booth was set up at the Pendleton Heritage Fair. Some nearby churches began requesting consignments of African goods for their local mission weekends.

Arlene and Barry Callen

A veteran African missionary of the Church of God (Anderson), J. Daniel Murrell, joined the Horizon family, raising his own support and helping to staff the gift shop.

The untimely death of Arlene Callen, wife of board member Barry Callen, came in March, 2003. In her honor, Barry made a contribution to establish the Arlene Callen Memorial Fund, an endowment intended to generate earnings that would keep replacing sold inventories of the gift shop in Pendleton and thus provide productive employment for disadvantaged Africans now related to Horizon's ministry. Since Arlene had a big missionary heart, this was a fitting and perpetual memorial.

The memorial fund would shift in focus in the years ahead. After an initial burst of excitement and local success, it became clear by early 2006 that the shop did not produce enough income to warrant the amount of expense and staff time required. So the board of directors decided to phase out this operation in its original form. The new form would be an internet gift shop on Horizon's web site, with many of the goods also sold at the concerts of the Kuyasa Kids Children's Choir, local church presentations, and the occasional Horizon banquets staged around the United States.

The purpose of the endowment dollars originally invested were moved, with Barry Callen's full blessing, to lay the foundation of Horizon's new University Scholarship Endowment Fund. Callen's long personal ministry in Christian higher education encouraged his support of the future education of select young Africans of high academic potential.

Just as the Clevengers were generous in providing space for the African Gift Shop in Pendleton, Indiana, so were they helpful in arranging affordable space for Horizon's home offices. The first office of Horizon was in the family room of Robert Pearson's home in rural

Pendleton. Especially after Joyce Chapple joined Horizon as a part-time staff person, the need for additional office space became obvious. Charles Clevenger, an active Christian businessman anxious to be a servant minister, says, "I knew that what Bob was doing was for the Lord, so again I tried to help out however I could." He owned pharmacies in Pendleton and nearby Anderson, a former bank building in Huntsville, the Falls Park Plaza in Pendleton, and other properties in the area. He and his wife Kelly, already having bought needed sewing machines for Africa, placed part of the former bank building in Huntsville in Horizon's hands at no cost for some months.

Especially when Samantha Morden (Frazier) and Mike Carey joined Horizon's staff, even more space was needed and soon was provided. Then later, as much more space was needed, Clevenger purchased a building across from Pendleton Heights High School and offered a large section of it to Horizon on a favorable financial basis. To date, this remains the center of Horizon's administrative operations in North America.

God often works in surprising ways, turning trials into triumphs. An example is Kelly Clevenger. An auto accident in 1989 forced a blood transfusion that carried into her body a disease that to this day is attacking her liver and threatening her life. Through no fault of her own, this trial has come. Then Horizon also came into her life. She learned of the millions of Africa's innocent children victimized by a terrible disease. Naturally, her heart went out to them, as has the Christian generosity of the Clevengers.

Horizon offices in Pendleton, Indiana

VISION TOURS AND WORK CAMPS

To really understand the desperate need of African AIDS orphans, to really reach the heart, an American living in such a different world needs to actually see and touch the human tragedy. If people could go to Africa and see firsthand the children and ministry possibilities, they likely would become involved through giving once they returned home. Therefore, early in Horizon's existence, there evolved the concept of Horizon hosting vision tours of Americans traveling to Africa. Some would also be work camps providing vital project services.

The first of these happened in February and March, 2003. Four persons from Indiana and four others from Colorado made the life-changing journey. A second such tour, this one including an independent group from North Coast Calvary Chapel in Carlsbad, California, continued to refurbish the Community Center in Kayamandi township, South Africa, and purchased basic equipment for a computer lab. Here was a committed congregation sponsoring numerous Horizon children, and now also working on the ground through one of Horizon's new partner organizations, *Kuyasa Horizon Empowerment.*

Such vision and work tours quickly became a vital means for Horizon to expose American Christians to the African need, often generating new donors, and accomplishing numerous tasks in the African ministry centers that could not be done any other way. In fact, many people who went became "repeaters" – they returned to Africa and took others with them. Personal experience kept turning into ministry expansion and donor support.

In the summer of 2005 alone, four traveling groups were planned under Horizon's umbrella. One was a group of fifteen from the First Church of God in Houston, Texas, led by pastor Don Bergstrom. The primary work would be construction of the first phase of a Drop-In Center for Horizon's approximately fifty orphans then being sponsored in Sekgopo Village, Limpopo Province, South Africa. A group of ten from Big Lake Church of God in Columbia City, Indiana, would be led by pastor Tim Kumfer and continue work in Sekgopo Village.

A group of ten from the Hillside Wesleyan Church in Cedar Rapids, Iowa, led by Jay and Teresa Davidson, would provide medical services in Sekgopo Village. Finally, there would be a Vision Tour from the Highland Park Community Church in Casper, Wyoming, led by Dorinda Jacobson, a volunteer facilitator of family missions at the church. Davidson, later to be a field representative for Horizon, reported that her African trip in 2005 "was the most profound experience of my life."

While Robert Pearson, Horizon's president, was still pastoring the Church of God congregation in Pendleton, Indiana, Todd Faulkner was a seminary student at nearby Anderson University School of Theology and serving as Pearson's pastoral associate. Faulkner had grandparents who had been missionaries in Sudan and Liberia. Their photos and stories had impacted his young life. Now, having heard much from Pearson about Horizon's ministries, he felt called to travel to Africa "to get more in touch with a piece of my own heritage." He had opportunity in November, 2006, to join Horizon's pastor's conferences in Zimbabwe and the Western Cape province of South Africa. He was inspired and would go back the following year to help lead a large pastor's conference in Uganda.

This pattern of going and then going again now has been repeated many times. People go to Horizon's ministry sites. They see, touch, taste, build, hold in their arms, have their hearts broken, and then go home different people. Their involvement with Horizon turns from interest and sympathy to active caring and concrete commitment. The following are three examples from among so very many.

On one African trip, a Horizon group collected money among themselves, bought the necessary materials, and then personally painted the full interior of the most important facility of the Sepedi tribe in Sekgopo Village in South Africa. This village had been off limits to whites during the apartheid era. Now the tribal leaders watched a group of American Whites, people who had taken their vacations and paid their own way to Africa. They were working hard, very hard, on behalf of Blacks in great need. The unusual sight was a powerful symbol to the tribal leaders. The next day these African leaders decided to respond. They sponsored a huge village party as a way of celebrating this amazing ministry of true togetherness and Christian service.

In 2004, president Robert Pearson made his second trip with an American group to the Mt. Darwin area of Zimbabwe, a remote region toward the border of Mozambique. Only one Christian congregation then existed in the thirty wards of this very rural area (each ward was about ten square kilometers). It was pastored by an AIDS orphan who had grown up in the home of Horizon's Tatenda and Lucia Gunguwo (see much about them in chapter six). One day during this 2004 visit, Tatenda organized a public walk with orphans and caregivers, with photos being taken. Large crowds gathered to watch and maybe receive food or become sponsored children themselves (various rumors had preceded the visitors). Since it was a Sunday morning and people expected the visitors to do something other than just take pictures, Pearson and Teresa Davidson started preaching along the way.

What could happen in such desolate circumstances? Well, more happened than was thought possible. That day three new congregations were founded. One ward leader, a communist, commented favorably to Pearson on what was being done by Horizon for the local people. He was surprised that Americans were willing to come to such a place

There is no end to the lines of hurting and waiting children

without fear. Soon all ward leaders met and gave permission for churches to be planted through Horizon's orphan ministry in any or all of the wards – today there are many congregations there, each affiliated with Eternal Word Ministries (Horizon's partner), and each involved in orphan care ministry.

Jason Pierantoni, at the time a ten-year-old boy from the Highland Park Community Church in Casper, Wyoming, went on a Horizon trip. Once having seen the great need in South Africa, he said to Horizon's president Pearson, "Uncle Bob, God told me to raise the money to pay for the needed well at Sekgopo Village. Here's how I am to do it when I get home. At my school I will ask the principal for permission to have all the kids bring money for each of the four weeks leading up to World AIDS Day (pennies and nickels the first week, dimes the second week, quarters the third week, with the big money during week four). Jason did just that, got the permission, and raised over $3,000!

Jason Pierantoni

In a worship service, Jason's pastor, John Spear, told the story of the boy's fundraising, saying that it was one of the most compelling missions stories he knew. Now this story would not end with one young man's inspired work. After it had been reported to the congregation, and realizing that the well for Sekgopo Village would require more than the $3,000, the congregation proceeded to give the rest! Several young persons in that congregation in addition to Jason, impacted by Horizon's vision, faith, and ministry, have reported their hopes for the future. They are likely to become missionaries themselves, with Jason hoping to be a medical doctor serving in Africa some day.

It has happened again and again. Actually seeing and touching the great need fires the heart and changes lives, first in Africa and then back in the United States. The God who calls also provides.

GUIDED BY NUMBERS 11

So much was happening for Horizon International in its beginning years. Much of it had to be in the United States in order to make possible actual ministry in Africa. People were inspired to participate, travel, and give, and ministry doors kept opening. The need was so great and God obviously was calling. The question that seemed so persistent, especially for Horizon's board of directors and corporate officers, was, "How can we finance all of this?" The answer began coming in part from the several new program efforts detailed above and the many persons catching the vision and sharing their time, work, and dollars. But somehow there had to be more, much more.

God was guiding Horizon into a massive task that required massive support. The need certainly was far beyond the modest resources that Horizon had in hand. However, reminded president Pearson in a devotional he shared with the board of directors on March 24, 2005, *nothing is beyond divine resources!* He recalled a comment attributed to Lloyd Ogilvie: "Where God guides, he provides." God clearly was granting an ever-expanding vision. Thus, said Pearson, "let us trust him to supply the resources we need to walk through the doors which God is opening." After all, according to Revelation 3:7, "What he opens no one can shut, and what he shuts no one can open."

Pearson continued that devotional by referring the board members to chapter eleven of the book of Numbers. The Hebrew people were complaining about having to eat manna all the time. Hearing their complaints, God promised Moses that the people would have enough meat to eat for a whole month. Moses measured this promise from a human perspective. Counting the vast number of people and the meager number of animals and fish in sight, he questioned God's ability to fulfill the promise. God answered the doubts of Moses with a discerning question – "Is the Lord's arm too short?" (Num. 11:23).

Is God's mouth bigger than his arms are long and strong? The answer was soon reported. The Lord drove a large flock of quail in from the sea. Reads Numbers 11:32, "All that day and night and all the next day the people went out and gathered quail." There was meat in abundance. There was no length or strength issue related to God's arm!

Near Christmas, 2007, Robert Pearson was alerted by a friend that there was a man in Tennessee who had interest in Horizon's ministry. He was a man of considerable resources who had been especially impressed by the story of Tatenda and Lucia Gunguwo in Zimbabwe that he had heard briefly. The friend said that this man might be willing to make a major gift to Horizon if contacted immediately. Pearson called quickly. The man answered and soon committed over the phone $150,000 for child sponsorships and projects in Zimbabwe, especially an administrative and counseling center yet to be established. This major gift came unexpectedly from a person previously unknown to Horizon, a clear example of the strong arm of the Lord. When meat was needed by God's people, somehow it showed up in abundance!

Horizon was a very young Christian ministry organization. Numerous doors already had opened, apparently by divine initiative. Board members wondered how quickly Horizon should expand as a ministry organization? Should its economic roots go deeply before branching out widely? Or might branching out be the only means for roots to ever go deeply? God certainly expected Horizon leaders to use discernment and caution; but God also was calling, and seemingly asking, "Is the Lord's arm too short?" Horizon leaders were answering with a firm "No!" Open doors would be walked through. Nothing inspired by God lies beyond divine resources.

For Horizon International, the first years of the new millennium were standing wide open for fruitful ministry in desperate African circumstances. The call was to march forward – forward to South Africa, and then into Zimbabwe, and then beyond to Uganda, Zambia, and Kenya. A world of AIDS orphans was waiting. For the children, there would be no future unless hope rose unexpectedly over their horizon. A ministry with the "horizon" name was determined to be that future for them, God willing.

Chapter Five

GATEWAY TO SUB-SAHARAN AFRICA

Start-up finances for Horizon International had begun flowing well by 2003. While a significant beginning, each day and each new ministry opportunity was a fresh challenge, a cause for seeking new donors and exercising more faith. Everything was needed – and all at once, it seemed. The board of directors gave guidance and president Robert Pearson worked constantly on the administrative and fundraising fronts.

The ministry was maturing and linking with many new partners. The Western Cape Province of South Africa was proving to be a crucial area of ministry beginnings for Horizon; it also was becoming an excellent gateway to additional ministry opportunities in sub-Saharan Africa. The AIDS menace did not respect national boundaries, boundaries that Horizon also would have to begin crossing.

On three occasions between 2002 and 2004, Jenny Carstens reached Florida from South Africa by traveling with the International Sports Coalition that her husband Cassie was helping to lead. Each time Horizon would pay her way to the west coast where she, her husband, and Robert Pearson would do church networking and fundraising together. It was during these trips that Horizon developed new relationships with several large congregations, and deepened a previous relationship with North Coast Calvary Chapel that already had a working arrangement with Cassie and Jenny Carstens in South Africa.

By 2005, the Kuyasa Kids choir from South Africa (see below) would be touring the United States for Horizon, greatly enhancing the visibility of Horizon's young ministry across the country. The choir was children ministering on behalf of other children, mostly by encouraging new child sponsorships.

So much was happening in the South African ministry and in the North American support system of Horizon in the first years of the new millennium. God obviously was in this ministry. Somehow, the administrative detail would get handled and adequate finances would be found. When God calls, God provides. The early ministry was expanding rapidly in the Kayamandi township near Capetown, South Africa. The ministry also, and very soon, would be moving into new organizational partnerships, and even into other parts of Africa.

RAPID PROGRESS IN KAYAMANDI

When Horizon launched its African ministry in the Western Cape Province of South Africa in November, 2001, primarily through its relationship with Cassie and Jenny Carstens, it was not fully aware of the strategic value of this move. There certainly was awareness of the alarming HIV/AIDS infection rate in the Xhosa townships of the Western Cape (as high as 40%!); there was less awareness that the Cape, and the city of Capetown in particular, was also a natural gateway to the rest of sub-Saharan Africa. That fact would prove a great blessing to Horizon.

Capetown is one of the more popular tourist attractions in the world. It also is a jumping off point for many North American mission groups attracted by the location, beauty, transportation, and relative social and political stability of the area. In the summer of 2004 alone, Horizon's partner organization, *Kuyasa Horizon Empowerment*, hosted work camps from Willow Creek Church in Chicago, Illinois, Mariners Church in

KUYASA
Horizon Empowerment

Newport Beach, California, and North Coast Calvary Chapel in Carlsbad, California. These were some of the largest Protestant congregations in the United States.

The Kayamandi township near the city of Stellenbosch in the Western Cape was the initial African ministry site of Horizon. It is home for about 30,000 members of the Xhosa tribe. With Horizon's ministry there only a year old, events already were moving quickly. President Pearson's report to Horizon's board of directors on December 19, 2002, made a series of exciting announcements. Twenty-five orphans were now fully sponsored there. What was equally exciting was that the ministry's local infrastructure was developing well and enabling the effective delivery of services to these children and many more likely to be served in the near future.

Five developments were worthy of particular note by the board of directors in that December and subsequent meetings.

1. A local legal entity was needed as the framework in and through which property could be held and programs conducted. Horizon conceived and funded the formation of a new South African not-for-profit corporation called *Kuyasa Horizon Empowerment*. A seven-member board of directors was named to give local direction to ministries such as the immediate care of AIDS orphans. By June, 2006, *Kuyasa Horizon Empowerment's* ministering staff included Jenny Carstens, project director, Cassie Carstens, leadership facilitator, Victor Mayataza, leadership development facilitator, Pumla Qalinge, Children's Program Coordinator, Mbongeni Mtshali, youth worker, and L'Atella Terrblanche, office manager.

2. A local office for Horizon's partner affiliate, *Kuyasa Horizon Empowerment*, was opened in a former bar near the Kayamandi Community Center. Beyond the office, a bakery and store for the sewing center were opened, offering more local employment.

3. The Stellenbosch City Council finally agreed to sell to Horizon's affiliate, *Kuyasa Horizon Empowerment*, the Kayamandi Community Hall. It would become the place from which ministry services in this key township could be concentrated. The location was excellent and the price reasonable, $9,800 (U.S.). Donors came forward to supply Horizon with this money, and an additional $12,700 for the facility's necessary

renovation and furnishing, including a small computer lab. A subsequent fire and legal complications rendered *Kuyasa Horizon Empowerment* the possessor but not yet the technical owner of this property. The purchase money remained in a South African trust for this eventual use. Complications or not, the ministry had a workable base and proceeded to function and expand.

The Hall was dedicated on March 3, 2003, before an enthusiastic crowd of about one hundred community, religious, and civic leaders. The speakers included Horizon staff, the principal of Kayamandi High School, local pastors, and the mayor of Stellenbosch. Members of the first Vision Tour of Horizon were there, including Robert Pearson, Horizon's president, Eric Dwiggins, member of the board of directors, Bonnie Powlison, future member of Horizon's board of directors, and Joyce Chapple, the first Horizon child sponsorship coordinator in the United States. Several key contacts were made at this event that would have future significance. The former Strongyard Hall was now dedicated as the Community Hall of what shortly would be Horizon's partner organization, *Kuyasa Horizon Empowerment*. It would be used in God's service on behalf of local orphaned children. It was being managed by Victor Mayataza, former mayor of Kayamandi.

The summer of 2003 brought a near tragedy that soon produced an unexpected silver lining. Once the Community Hall was secured from the Stellenbosch City Council, squatter shacks appeared around and even attached to its cement-block walls. This kept the final transfer of ownership from being completed. According to Xhosa culture and local law, a shack left unchallenged for twenty-four hours cannot be moved. The insurance company would not cover the property for Horizon because of the problem shacks. So, the City Council continued as the technical owner and negotiations continued with the shack owners, while Horizon's purchase money was put in trust and its ministry proceeded in and from the facility.

Then something else happened. Fire! A blaze raged one day, destroying numerous shack homes in Kayamandi, including the ones troubling the front of the Community Hall, which itself sustained significant damage. This sad situation, ironically, cleared the way for the likely transfer of the ownership of the facility to Horizon's ministry partner in Kayamandi. A blocking perimeter was rapidly built to keep new shacks from appearing. The insurance paid for the Hall's repairs, making the place better than before. Then came another twist. The Stellenbosch City Council realized that the facility sits on tribal lands and thus could be "awarded" but not sold – so the Council provided the Hall's full use in perpetuity, but continues to be the legal owner, covering select overhead costs.

By December of 2005, with repairs and improvements of the Hall complete, the programming of *Kuyasa Horizon Empowerment* in Kayamandi township was extensive. There were weekly classes for English as a second language and basic computer skills (seven computers had been donated by North Coast Calvary Chapel, while the supporting software had been given by Mariners Church in California). The program *Sports Center One* had been launched that October in the Hall, with Joshua Phalwane serving as sports coordinator. Activities ranged from basketball and soccer to ballroom dancing and weight training.

A gift of land and facilities in Kayamandi township was made to *Kuyasa Horizon Empowerment* in 2006 by the Stellenbosch City Council. It included the original Kayamandi farmhouse and winery, greatly expanding the physical base of operation for this first ministry location of Horizon in Africa. The plan set in motion was for the farmhouse to become the home of administrative offices for *Kuyasa Horizon Empowerment*, with the former winery to be the hub of orphan skill training and other ministries. God had new uses for old things.

4. Local Kayamandi women needed employment. In fact, about one-half of the township's adults were unemployed. Horizon donors made it possible to purchase ten commercial sewing machines for them to make clothes for them-selves and their families. But that was only the beginning of the sewing work. The vision included making and selling clothes for

Jenny Carstens teaching at sewing center

income. Kuyasa's sewing school began in July, 2002, with twenty-five women enrolled. Then it opened the Kuyasa Sewing Factory. In November, 2002, a contract was awarded to make school uniforms for Kayamandi High School, allowing the employment of eleven of its school's recent graduates. Money was raised to buy more equipment for the factory to do quality work.

Local curio shops began asking for Xhosa products and, back in the United States, Horizon's new *Out of Africa Gift Shop* needed inventory (see chapter four), and the Pendleton, Indiana, Church of God congregation needed new baptismal robes. All would be provided gladly from across the Atlantic Ocean. By 2004, there was fundraising going on for a new Welding School to join the Kuyasa Sewing School and Factory. Also in Kayamandi township, a new bakery had just opened. This and the other endeavors were intended to transform a community where Horizon's orphans were living. It was taking seriously the old adage, "Give them fish and feed them for a day; teach them to fish and feed them for a lifetime!" If it "takes a village" to rear a child it certainly would take various elements of life in Kayamandi township to care for the orphans properly.

5. Money was raised in the United States to fund the partner team on the ground in South Africa – initially, Jenny Carstens, Horizon's community networker/organizer and her full-time administrative assistant, Isabel Barendse, a senior at the nearby University of Stellenbosch. Pumla Qalinge then was added to the Kayamandi staff, allowing much-needed counseling with orphans in their native Xhosa language. A grant came from the *Jesus Is Love Foundation* in San Diego, California. Cindy Nixon (originally an Horizon intern in 2005) became the Learning Center Manager, and Pumla Qalinge the Children's Program Coordinator. She had been on the ministry team since September, 2003.

THE KUYASA KIDS: NEVER GIVE UP!

A most memorable Christmas was experienced by Robert Pearson in 2003. He was traveling alone to South Africa for ten days of administrative meetings. Mechanical failure related to his flight in

Atlanta, Georgia, delayed his African arrival and forced the rescheduling of something he had not expected in the first place. God surely was in this delay.

When his plane finally touched down, Pearson was met and taken directly to an elementary school in Kayamandi township. There he was treated to the singing of an informal children's choir comprised of about twenty-five orphaned children gathered hastily over their lunch hour just to sing for him. They sang several songs in "Pinky's" public school classroom, including the song "Never Give Up!" It was their way of greeting and thanking Pearson for Horizon's vital ministry to them.

Pearson would say this to Horizon donors in a March, 2004, letter: "Seldom in life have I felt the emotions that welled up within me in these moments!" He went on to report his new dream of bringing a Horizon orphan choir to the United States in 2005. Could donors prayerfully consider making such a major undertaking possible? Yes, it would be very expensive and difficult to implement. Even so, its potential for stimulating new child sponsorships was substantial.

These African children had learned that rousing song about never giving up while attending a recent summer Adventure Camp that Horizon had made possible, and where many of them had committed their lives to Jesus Christ. Facing difficult odds in life, but now with Horizon on their side, virtually their parent, and with Jesus Christ in their hearts, they had gained courage, and obviously were becoming brothers and sisters to each other. They certainly had an ear-pleasing way of thanking their American "father" and expressing their new resolve to face life with fresh hope and determination. Their potential musical ministry and Christian witness among North Americans could generate considerable enthusiasm and awareness, likely adding to the list of active donors ready to link hands and dollars in the service of many more desperate children.

Mbongeni Mtshali

An exceptional South African young man, Mbongeni Mtshali, emerged as Kuyasa's youth worker in Kayamandi township. He also was the founder in 2004 and the continuing inspirational leader of what soon was being called the Kuyasa Kids Children's Choir. A gifted linguist with a brief theatrical career in Johannesburg, South Africa, he has directed the music, dance, and choreography of the concerts of the Kuyasa Kids from the group's beginning. Even more, he has been the spiritual and recreational leader of the afternoon Children's Club and facilitator of the Adventure Camps of Kayamandi (see chapter eight).

Especially inspiring and promising was the sheer energy and Christian faith of the members of the Kuyasa Kids choir, faith in themselves, in each other, and in their God. One of the children, Confidence, would become president Pearson's own special "daughter" in Africa. In an important sense, however, these were all "his kids." They affectionately call him "Uncle Bob."

Pearson, deeply moved by what he saw and felt when he heard these children sing, quickly realized that this group was capable of inspiring many people, maybe even in the United States.

Pearson and Confidence

Thus, he recommended to Horizon's board of directors, in its meeting of January 30, 2005, that the board recognize the ministry of the African children's choir and authorize its travel abroad as representatives of Horizon International. Such an experience would be life-changing for the children and open doors to major congregations, possibly generating numerous new child sponsorships.

The board of directors agreed to plans for a first tour in the spring of 2005, involving nineteen musically gifted orphans from Kayamandi township, including a small African dance team. They would be accompanied by supervising adults and be known as the *Kuyasa Kids Children's Choir*. In the Xhosa language, "kuyasa" means "sun rising."

Such was the case in the rescued lives of these special children. It was hoped that, through their travel and singing, new resources would come, enabling the sun to rise in the lives of many more AIDS orphans. The gifted children could help other children, a way of giving thanks and giving back, passing on the blessing.

The cost for such an American tour was very high, more than $30,000 just for airfares, but it was judged that the investment was worth the risk. The mayor of the city of Stellenbosch in the Western Cape, Willie Ortell, assisted with funds from the youth development fund of his municipality budget. A $20,000 grant from a foundation in the United States helped buy the tickets. And then, surely by God's grace, help came from a world-famous musical group. God often acts in surprising ways!

The name of this American rock band is *Switchfoot*, a group honored with Dove Awards and often featured at large Christian festivals around the world. This band was in South Africa, went to Kayamandi township, heard the Kuyasa Kids sing, and were moved to start *Lowercase People*, a quarterly online magazine for music, arts, and social justice. They also produced "Kuyasa Kids: Live in Kayamandi," a CD which could be taken to American congregations and sold wherever the Kuyasa Kids would sing. In fact, its inventory soon was sold out, with a profit of $15,000 that was put in the University Scholarship Fund of Horizon's affiliate, *Kuyasa Horizon Empowerment*, especially for children in Kayamandi township, Western Cape Province, South Africa.

There was more. The impact of touring the South African townships and encountering the Kuyasa Kids inspired *Switchfoot* to write the song they called "The Shadow Proves the Sunshine." It appeared in the album *Nothing Is Sound*. Four lines of this song capture the heart-cry of AIDS orphans – and also the mission of Horizon International:

> *Oh, Lord, why did you forsake me?*
> *Oh, Lord, don't be far away, away.*
> *Storm clouds gathering beside me,*
> *Please Lord, don't look the other way.*

The Kuyasa Kids Children's Choir

Echoing this heart-cry was what had become the theme song of the Kuyasa Kids. It was "Never Give Up!" The words of the title are repeated numerous times throughout the song, supplemented with proud bodily movements and facial expressions that send a clear message. "In times of sorrow, in times of sorrow, in times of sorrow, in times of sorrow, you must never, never, never, never, never, never, never give up!" By faith, through Horizon, and by God's grace, a growing number of orphans would now never give up!

It finally happened. The Kuyasa Kids flew on April 21, 2005, to Atlanta, Georgia, to begin a three-week tour. They would perform thirty-three times before a total of some 50,000 people in Georgia, Florida, Texas, and California. They sang, danced, and testified for several of the larger congregations in the United States and, while in Miami, Florida, for the national staff of the Burger King corporation. This fast-food chain had decided to help with the tour. One result of this first American tour was the sponsoring of 180 new African orphans – orphans now helping orphans! The tour cost totaled $85,000 and was fully covered by generous donations. This was a miracle that would make other miracles possible.

The second U. S. tour came in September and October of 2006 and focused on locations in Illinois, Indiana, and Ohio. Especially featured this time were concert appearances of the choir before the student bodies of

Anderson University, Huntington University, and Taylor University in Indiana. The primary purpose remained the recruitment of new child sponsors. The result of this second tour was the sponsoring of 224 new African children. Looking ahead to see how a third tour could be funded, Robert Pearson set up five tour teams of donor categories. One qualified to join the Zebra team with any gift up to $249. Increasing levels included the Giraffe, Rhino, and Elephant teams, culminating in membership in the Lion team for a gift of $5,000 or more. The great animals of Africa were opening American hearts.

The itinerary for the early fall tour of 2007 began with long flights from Capetown, South Africa, to Los Angeles, California. A series of concerts found the Kuyasa Kids inspiring crowds of Americans at North Coast Calvary Chapel (Carlsbad, CA), Crossroads Community Church

North American Concert Tours
KUYASA KIDS CHILDREN'S CHOIR OF HORIZON INTERNATIONAL
Kayamandi, South Africa

Years	Months	Concert Highlights
2005	April-May	California, Georgia, Florida, Texas. The orphans sang and danced in thirty-three settings before a total of some 50,000 people.
2006	Sept.-Oct.	Indiana, Illinois, and Ohio. Nine congregations, one high school, and three universities (Anderson, Huntington, Taylor)
2007	Sept.-Oct.	Arizona, California, Colorado, and Wyoming. Twelve congregations, the Art Peace Gallery in Burbank, CA, and one university (Azusa Pacific)
2008	Mar.-April	Indiana, Michigan, Ohio, Pennsylvania, and Virginia. Twelve congregations and one college (Malone)
2009	April 4-26	California, Illinois, Oregon, Washington. One college (Warner Pacific) and fourteen congregations, including the large Willow Creek Community Church in Chicago, Ill.

(Yuba City, CA), North Hills Community Church (Phoenix, AZ), McDowell Mountain Community Church (Scottsdale, AZ), with additional appearances at Azusa Pacific University, Highland Park Community Church (Casper, WY), and elsewhere.

Highlights of the first five tours are summarized on page 119. The excitement and benefits of these concerts can hardly be reduced to words and numbers on paper! One number, however, is significant. By 2009, the tours of the children had stimulated the sponsorship of some 1,000 African children! Only eternity can begin to comprehend the wonder of this accomplishment.

Kuyasa Kids celebrating health and Christian joy

MANY NEW PARTNERSHIPS

The various ministries now well begun in the Kayamandi township near Stellenbosch, South Africa, soon encouraged similar beginnings elsewhere. For instance, Langa township is one of the oldest in the Western Cape Province. In March, 2005, Cecelia Elrick and Joan Gerard, Christians living nearby, launched a weekly women's Bible study there. It soon was obvious that several of the older women were having to care for grandchildren who had lost their parents to AIDS. Elrick and Gerard visited Jenny Carstens to see what might be done, leading to Horizon's involvement with a child sponsorship ministry, a weekly women's Bible study, a needlework class, and an afternoon children's club.

A very large Black township, Bloekombos, is a place where Jenny Carstens prepared the way, meeting with township pastors and identifying five orphans ready for sponsorship under a home-based care model similar to Kayamandi's. Horizon decided to partner with *Sarfat*, a Bloekombos-based community development organization. A community hall facility, unfinished and owned by *Sarfat*, would be made available for Horizon's use, with Horizon seeking major funding to complete its construction. Work camps would be planned, enabling an important center for future Horizon ministries in Bloekombos. They would build on the foundational work financed in 2006 by Trinity Methodist Church in Chelmsford, England. Surita Cillie and Leonie van Rooyen were on the scene, and now as Horizon's project directors.

In addition to these new township ministries, other important new partnerships also developed, expanding Horizon's ministries in new and cooperative ways. For instance, in September, 2003, a contact of Jenny Carstens led to a new partnership. Noluthando School for the Deaf ministers to young Africans who, because of their disability, find it very difficult to function in normal society. Some of these children (about 20 of 176) were also disadvantaged because they were AIDS orphans.

At the time, Noluthando was a Christian-based school in Khayalitsha township, home to over a million people east of Capetown. A partnership with Horizon was formed and enthusiastically endorsed by Horizon's board of directors. It led to almost immediate sponsorship of six of the students, beginning with the younger ones. One of the teachers,

Ina Calitz

Christopher Galada

Ina Calitz, became one of two Horizon project directors at Noluthando. The other was Kunjelwa Vodwana.

President Robert Pearson said to Horizon's board of directors that "future Vision Tour visits to Khayalitsha will melt the heart of the most hardened North American." In the January, 2004, donor letter, he referred to Noluthando as "an oasis of hope in the poverty of Khayalitsha township. It isn't the kind of place you would want to raise your kids. Without Noluthando, however, Khayalitsha's hearing impaired orphans wouldn't have a chance!"

In early 2004, president Pearson made two trips to visit Northland – A Church Distributed, located in Longwood, Florida. This congregation of some 10,000 people had been building a relationship with a large Dutch Reformed Church in Capetown called *Vredelust*, where Cassie Carstens is an associate pastor. Pearson preached in this church on August 8, 2004. Afterwards, the pastor, Leon Oosthuisen, met with Pearson in Khayalitsha to visit a church and conclude an agreement to partner with Horizon in sponsoring AIDS orphans in Khayalitsha. Thomas and Thembie Thamaga, senior pastors of the church, would serve as project directors through the Aids Prevention Outreach Center. While in Capetown that very week, pastor Oosthuisen presented the visiting delegation from Northland church in Florida with a mission partnership agreement for Khayalitsha that named Horizon as the AIDS orphan provider.

Major doors seemed to be opening, and with them came new questions. Caring for the immediate needs of orphans was the first Horizon preoccupation. But a nagging reality had to be addressed. What

Sponsored children at Noluthando School

about the negative social environments in which the orphans lived, settings so ready to undo whatever good is done? If communities are not transformed, only caring for the children during their youth might be delaying the inevitable – their becoming HIV infected at an older age because of crime and lack of employment. Robert Pearson and Cassie Carstens were already discussing the need for a school of community transformation. The need was becoming a vision ready for reality.

In 2004 this vision found a way of becoming real. A Horizon Vision Tour that year included participants Cindy Nixon and Samantha Morden (Frazier), both future leaders of Horizon. They attended the opening ceremonies of the first class of the African Leadership Institute for Community Transformation (ALICT), which included twenty-three Christian leaders from twelve African countries. The Horizon board of directors then authorized in August, 2004, a formal working relationship between Horizon and ALICT.

The school's field work would take place through the *Kuyasa Horizon Empowerment's* center in Kayamandi. Jenny Carstens would teach part-time at the school on AIDS orphan care. Contact with these students could be a means for Horizon to expand across the African continent in years to come. At a minimum, new Horizon coordinators and interns could gain valuable training experience through ALICT.

All of this growth in Horizon's ministries and partnerships in the Western Cape Province of South Africa brought changing roles for the Carstens. Originally, Cassie was the Southern Africa Director, with Jenny the South African Coordinator. Now that the developing strategic ministry centers were staffed by regional coordinators, Cassie and Jenny began to serve as African Consultants for Horizon and its affiliated ministry partners, along with their ongoing assignment as regional coordinators in the Western Cape.

It also had come time for formal organizational development on African soil. Since its inception in the Western Cape, Horizon had been operating as an entity under another Christian non-profit ministry, *Rigters Opleiding*. Horizon, sensitive to its grassroots-up philosophy of operation, began moving toward the formation of a local Christian non-profit organization in Kayamandi. It soon was formally established. The Kayamandi Community Hall and other properties and ministries would be held by and operated through this new entity. It would be known as *Kuyasa Horizon Empowerment*.

As Horizon's ministry began to take shape in Limpopo Province, South Africa, hours by car from Kayamandi and a very different place, a similar new legal entity would be formed and called *Horizon Thusanang*.

ALICT, 2005

BEYOND THE WESTERN CAPE

Limpopo is the most northern district of South Africa, named after the great river that flows along its northern border. Its neighbors are Botswana, Mozambique, and Zimbabwe, and it features the world-famous Krueger National Park. Bob and Bonnie Powlison were key Horizon supporters from Colorado (Bonnie later would be a member of the Horizon board of directors). They had put president Robert Pearson in touch with Juan and Engela DeVilliers. Juan was a medical surgeon and landowner in Limpopo. Engela owned and operated a private elementary school. They were interested in serving the needs of AIDS orphans. Pearson made contact and Dr. DeVilliers shared their vision and willingness to begin working with Horizon.

In March, 2003, Juan and Engela DeVilliers hosted a meeting of pastors, school administrators, and social workers to discuss the possible launching of a local Horizon ministry for AIDS orphans in Limpopo Province – many of them lived in a series of tribal villages. In addition to president Pearson, board member Eric Dwiggins was present at the original meeting. From this meeting came firm recommendations from president Pearson that soon were fully affirmed by Horizon's board of directors back in the United States.

A home-based orphan care ministry would be launched. The work would be coordinated from the DeVilliers' farm, with the first twenty-five sponsored orphans to come from nearby Kgapane Village. The Limpopo regional coordinators would be Andries and Nelly van der Merwe, veteran Dutch Reformed missionaries with a strong business background and divine call to make a difference for AIDS orphans. American sponsors were soon found for twenty-nine children.

The new organization, *Horizon Thusanang*, was formed – "thusanang" is the Sepedi word for "helping hands." A local board was named to direct this body, with Juan DeVilliers functioning initially as its chair. A philosophic struggle soon followed, unfortunate in one way, and yet leading to a clarification of mission strategy. Should the ministry bring orphans from their villages to the school on the DeVillier's farm for educational purposes (the desire of Engela DeVilliers), or should the

Horizon Thusanang board of directors, 2005

focus of the ministry be in the villages themselves, functioning in a variety of ways, including and extending beyond education? The decision, "a God decision" reports president Pearson, was to keep the children in their villages, thinking of community transformation as a key to total orphan care.

Wonderful things soon followed this key strategy decision. By 2006, the inspired ministry of *Horizon Thusanang* in Limpopo Province, led by Andries and Nelly van der Merwe, was granted the "Non-Profit Excellence Award," a major achievement for a very young ministry organization affiliated with Horizon International. The Horizon board of directors in the United States had formally approved the van der Merwes as regional coordinators for Limpopo Province and recognized the newly formed local board.

The van der Merwes, exceptional Christian leaders, initially served half-time with Horizon and also continued sponsoring AIDS-education workshops in the province through *World Teach*. Fundraising began in order to cover salary expenses for the new coordinators. A delivery system was devised to enable routine distribution of food and clothing to sponsored children, and to generally supervise their well being.

Nelly and Andries van der Merwe

The Horizon ministry, under the supervision of the van der Merwes, would quickly expand to serve over four hundred orphaned kids in twenty-one Sepedi villages in the Lataba Subdistrict of Limpopo Province, South Africa. Additional staff people were added to the ministry – an administrative assistant, accountant, food parcels coordinator, and an array of American interns and South African volunteers over the years to come. By 2009, the food parcel ministry had outgrown the van der Merwe's garage and funds were being raised in North America to rent and remodel a nearby warehouse.

Andries van der Merwe in the food distribution center

Another significant development emerged from that first exploratory trip into Limpopo Province in March, 2003. A location was sought for a brief safari experience for the American travelers. The DeVilliers recommended the property of some friends, Boetlap and Dalene Pohl, who were living on a tomato farm and hosting friends for tours of the large property where many animals lived. These people were well known to the van der Merwes. The Horizon Vision Tour group went there and rode on four-wheelers among the amazing animals. The group included Robert Pearson (Horizon president), Joyce Chapple (first child sponsor coordinator of Horizon), Eric Dwiggins (one of the four founding board members of Horizon), and Bonnie Powlison (later a Horizon board member and treasurer).

Robert Pearson said to the Pohls that he would bring numerous American groups to visit them if they would build a lodge where they could stay for brief periods of time. Largely from this encouragement, a

Boetlap and Dalene Pohl

wonderful set of lodge facilities were soon built and Horizon International did become the best "customer" of the Pohls – in fact, more like family. These people and this wonderful place, now called Magnab Safari Lodge, grew to become part of the Horizon ministry team in Limpopo, with Pearson becoming an "uncle" to the three Pohl girls. Even though by 2009 the property had been sold to a Black empowerment company, the Pohls have stayed on as managers and special friends of Horizon and its ministries in that region.

By January, 2004, the Limpopo ministry had expanded into Sekgopo Village, home of over 30,000 people. Soon the Sepedi tribal chief and her council in Sekgopo Village gave a large piece of property to *Horizon Thusanang*, with the South African government financing the salaries of a team of home care hospice nurses, employees of *Horizon Thusanang*. Still ahead would be the development of a major orphan drop-in center, to be the pride of the area. By 2009, nearly two hundred orphans in this one village would be under Horizon care. Also, in July of 2009, a major grant was received from an agency related to the South African government. It enabled the completion of all phases of the Sekgopo Drop-In Center, including kitchen equipment, a computer training center, a four-

Morris Walter at the Magnab Safari Lodge

Sekgopo Drop-In Center

teen-seat mini bus, and more – one of the best things ever to happen for *Horizon Thusanang's* efforts in South Africa.

Several pastors in the United States expressed interest in tithing to Horizon the proceeds from their church building funds. One was Timothy Kumfer of the Big Lake Church of God in Columbia City, Indiana. He had accompanied president Pearson on an administrative trip to southern Africa in July, 2003, and later would emerge as a volunteer field representative for Horizon in the United States. Another congregation that made a similar tithing commitment and now has followed through with it is the Northview Christian Life Church of Carmel, Indiana.

By the summer of 2004, enough child sponsorships had been gained for Limpopo Province to allow the van der Merwes to move to full-time status with Horizon. Sponsored orphans by then lived in multiple locations, including Sekgosese and Sekgopo Villages. While the work expanded in Africa, building relationships and securing funding remained a central task back in the United States. Therefore, the van der Merwes traveled in 2006 to speak in the Faith Promise Mission Weekend of the First Church of God in Houston, Texas. They then traveled to other American locations supporting them, finally coming to Indiana to meet with Horizon's board of directors in February, 2006.

The board of directors was pleased to welcome these key Horizon partners. From them the members received extensive information about the ministries and needs in Limpopo Province. They then approved the adding of Adri van der Merwe, the daughter, to the staff of *Horizon Thusanang* in Limpopo Province, South Africa. Such was possible because of the growing generosity of particular donors. Key new American assistance was now

coming from Jay and Teresa Davidson of Cedar Rapids, Iowa. Jay, a general contractor, and Teresa, a nurse practitioner, determined to make regular trips to Limpopo Province to help coordinate Vision Tours and Work Camps sponsored by Horizon. Later, they would become Horizon field representatives in the states of Iowa and Wisconsin.

Jay and Teresa Davidson

In Limpopo Province, Sekgopo Village is especially poor, with an HIV infection rate of 50% and an unemployment rate of almost 80%. It was without safe drinking water when Horizon arrived. The tribal chief was thrilled to learn that an American businessman on Horizon's Vision Tour had volunteered to pay the necessary $2,500 to drill a new bore hole. Horizon proposed to build a multi-purpose orphan drop-in center, and was given assurance by the chief that prime land would be given to Horizon for that purpose. When the land was visited, it turned out to be large in size, more than expected, and fully adequate for the purpose. A work camp was planned to begin construction.

In the summer of 2005, Horizon was very busy in Sekgopo Village. The first phase of the drop-in center was built, a medical clinic was staffed by a team of American physicians and nurses, and daily ministry to sponsored orphans was now routine. American pastors came and made sexual abstinence presentations in fourteen public schools, resulting in 10,000 "Purity Cards" being signed by youth in Sekgopo Village. If the young could be convinced to refrain from sexual activity until marriage, and then be faithful to their spouses, the continuing spread of HIV/AIDS could be stopped to a significant degree.

Proudly displaying their purity cards

After a trip to South Africa with Horizon, Dan Pentecost made a big decision. He would take his passion for the sponsored children to a new level. On July 17, 2008, he actually moved to Moketsi, South Africa. Living on a family farm, he quickly became an invaluable aid to Andries and Nelly van der Merwe, Horizon's regional coordinators in Limpopo Province. Dan bought, sorted, and even helped deliver the food for Horizon's children in the area. He reported that he "really likes just hanging out with the kids." What a gift of life and love!

Horizon's ministry had been officially organized in Limpopo Province, South Africa, to enable local leadership of the ministry and formal government recognition. *Horizon Thusanang* had become the legal entity for Horizon International's ministries. To this legal entity soon came a major gift of land and buildings from the Duiwelskloof Roman Catholic diocese. There had been contact between Robert Pearson and Father Martin, a local Roman Catholic leader from Ireland and a longtime friend of Andries and Nelly van der Merwe.

Martin was aware of the area ministries of *Horizon Thusanang*. The priest's question to Pearson had been, "Would Horizon support orphaned children who were Catholic?" He was pleased at the affirmative response – he was used to conflict between Protestants and Catholics in Ireland. That would not be duplicated here, not by Horizon, and not at the expense of the children!

This key property was in one of the Sepedi villages, Matipane, where Horizon was sponsoring children. Including about fifty acres, this former "fair grounds" of the Sepedi tribe had a relatively new community hall with water and electricity, and it even had an outdoor amphitheater seating about 200 people. The potential uses of this property were numerous. Andries and Nelly van der Merwe soon were overseeing the feeding of eighty children three times per week in this community hall. Some were Roman Catholic – Father Martin had been kept informed and continued to be pleased. God's people were joining hands to do God's work.

Highland Park Community Church group from Wyoming

Matipane Drop-In Center

Other villages would open to Horizon, with children becoming sponsored and served through additional drop-in centers that would be built, usually through the labor and love of work camps of visiting Americans. One of the villages was Madumeleng.

In the summer of 2007, a door opened to Horizon in still another province of South Africa, assisted by David Coen of Mariners Church in California. He introduced Robert Pearson to Glynn Smith, a native South

Children at Madumeleng Drop-In Center

African active in Christian ministry. Smith, in turn, led Pearson to others. Having been authorized by Horizon's board of directors, Pearson visited and investigated new partnership possibilities in Richard's Bay, KwaZulu-Natal Province.

Richard's Bay is an important aluminum and coal port not far from the Durban International Airport. Pearson was introduced to two wonderful couples there who already were involved in orphan care ministries. Chadd and Kate Bain had founded Izulu Orphan Projects ("Izulu" means "heaven"), but could not proceed as desired because of lack of funding. A second orphan ministry in the area was having similar problems. These were needs that Horizon was positioned to meet.

Chadd and Kate Bain

Gavin and Elaine Charlton were heading a non-profit ministry called MusaweNkosi ("God's grace"). They were working with several Zulu pastors and congregations in the Richard's Bay vicinity and had built some children's homes. They also were having difficulty sustaining their work financially. These two situations fit well with Horizon's way of working through partners. It would come alongside these quality local leaders and provide the child sponsorship dollars needed to empower the existing ministries to be stable and effective.

Gavin and Elaine Charlton

The Village Church in Irvine, California, was already asking for the privilege of being the exclusive source of child sponsorships for Richard's Bay. Given the obvious need and this offer, Horizon's board of directors authorized on September 8, 2007, the implementation of a partnership with MusaweNkosi. Gavin and Elaine Charlton would serve as Horizon's project directors. And with Izulu Orphan Projects, Chadd and Kate Bain would serve as Horizon's project directors.

It was obvious that the future ministries of Horizon International, already in various South African locations and now even in Harare, Zimbabwe, would likely come to range even farther. The strategic value of the Western Cape base as a gateway to the rest of southern Africa continued to be obvious.

For instance, in 2004 groups from several American mega-churches were in the Capetown area. One group from Mariners Church of Newport Beach, California, spent a week in Kayamandi, with some of its people deciding to sponsor a total of ten orphans through Horizon. Mariners soon named Horizon its ministry of choice in South Africa. Bill Hybels, pastor of Willow Creek Church in Chicago, was a guest of Horizon's affiliated ministries in Kayamandi.

Being the gateway to all of southern Africa, the Capetown area of South Africa generated numerous contacts for Horizon. For instance, while Robert Pearson and Horizon's first Vision Tour group were in the city of Stellenbosch and Kayamandi township in February and March, 2003, Pearson had been approached by a Rev. Japhet Ndhlovu, General

Secretary of the Christian Council of Churches for the country of Zambia. He wanted Pearson and the Carstens to visit Zambia to explore AIDS ministry opportunities there.

Doors kept opening, leading to surprising and sometimes distant places of new ministry. Horizon, now well begun in South Africa, was poised to expand to other nations. The first, and one to be of particular significance and challenge, was Zimbabwe.

Chapter Six

CROSSING THE LIMPOPO

The AIDS pandemic stretched far beyond South Africa. So would the mission and ministries of Horizon International. Eventually, the people and resources of Horizon were making a major impact in South Africa's Western Cape, Limpopo, and Natal Provinces. But now there also came a crossing of the Limpopo River to the north. Beyond the border of South Africa lies another amazing land with an alarmingly high HIV infection rate, and with a man and wife already called of God to do something about it.

In God's providence, it was inevitable that the Gunguwo and Horizon families and ministries would meet and partner. God was calling from the pain of Zimbabwe, and Horizon was again hearing and "on the grow"! The years between 2002 and 2009 would be deeply troubled for Zimbabwe, but Horizon, through it all, would be there and stand faithfully with its ministry partners. A truly dramatic story was beginning to unfold, one with scenes scattered across four different areas of Zimbabwe. God was at work on behalf of children caught in the worst of human circumstances!

The Limpopo River forms the portion of the northern border of South Africa that separates it from Zimbabwe. This liquid national border was immortalized in the short story "The Elephant's Child" by British author Rudyard Kipling.

In his *Just So Stories*, this river is described as "the great grey-green, greasy Limpopo River, all set about with fever-trees," a place where the "bi-colored python rock-snake" dwells. There are also plenty of hippopotamuses playing and plundering as this waterway separates nations and wanders eastward toward the Indian Ocean.

In 1923 the European settlers living in the landlocked area bordered by Zambia, Mozambique, South Africa, and Botswana voted to be the self-governing British colony of Southern Rhodesia. Then in 1979 a big change came. Robert Mugabe led a guerrilla uprising and became president of what now was to be called Zimbabwe. Full national independence was achieved in 1980, bringing with it President Mugabe's controversial land distribution campaign. It soon caused most European farmers to depart. Commercial farming, once enabling this land to be known as the "Breadbasket of Central Africa," virtually ended.

Teresa Davidson, a nurse practitioner from Iowa, traveled to Zimbabwe with Horizon in 2005. She carried a quantity of medications with her for use with the locally ill and was concerned about a possible problem with customs officials. While the medications were cleared without difficulty, there was a shock awaiting her inside the country. She soon saw evident starvation, the "wasted farmland with a grip of death on its people." Traveling one day across the country, she asked a local Horizon leader why people were burning fields. She was told, "They are hunting mice to eat." It was some time before she could speak again. Her heart reached out to the children. She and her husband Jay began volunteering with Horizon, and by November of 2008 they were Horizon's field representatives for Iowa and Wisconsin.

Jay and Teresa Davidson

The human suffering, caused partly by government policy, was being compounded by circumstances largely outside of government control. There was drought and the rapid spread of the HIV/AIDS pandemic. All of this conspired to bring disease, hunger, an alarmingly high inflation rate, very high unemployment, many premature deaths, and some 800,000 orphans.

Peter Cunningham was one of the last White farmers to retain his land in Zimbabwe. In 1998 he began giving portions of the farm's resources (baby chickens and ostriches) to poor Black villagers living nearby. Mugabe's soldiers came in 2002 to seize the whole farm, but the villagers stood in the way and explained that this couldn't happen or all the people would suffer greatly. The soldiers finally backed away. Later, Cunningham, still retaining the farm, learned of Horizon's new work and offered a farmhouse and land for a new children's home, and even more later for an extensive children's village. The early focus of Horizon's ministry in Zimbabwe, however, would actually begin with others, also amazing people living in the nation's capital city, Harare.

A wonderful country had become a deeply troubled land. Even so, why would the new Horizon ministry, hardly well established yet in South Africa, venture across the Limpopo River into Zimbabwe? Sometimes things just seem to happen. It turns out, however, that in this case God was clearly guiding a process of ministry expansion. The river crossing for Horizon began in a strange place indeed, one far from Zimbabwe. It happened during an extended layover between flights in England's Gatwick Airport.

Michael Henderson was there in England in late November, 2001, on his way to Capetown, South Africa, to join Robert Pearson. By chance (or divine providence), Henderson encountered a woman named Lucia Gunguwo, also in transit. After some small talk, Lucia began reporting about her church-planting husband, Tatenda. They were supporting fifteen AIDS orphans in their little home in Harare, Zimbabwe, on very little income. This "chance" conversation in England is where Horizon International began its crossing of the Limpopo River into the needy land of Zimbabwe.

ORPHANS IN OUR HOME

Tatenda and Lucia Gunguwo embody in their own dramatic lives the tragedy, sacrifice, and selfless service to orphans that is at the heart of Horizon International. In fact, Tatenda was himself orphaned as a boy of twelve. Guerrillas led by Robert Mugabe were attacking the Southern Rhodesia government of Ian Smith. They came to the home of the Gunguwos and demanded that Tatenda's farmer father turn over his seven sons to them – presumably to be trained as rebel fighters. When he refused, he was slaughtered with a machete in front of his family. His wife died the next year, leaving all eleven of the children orphaned. Tatenda would be haunted by this horrible scene all of his life. Only by God's grace would he turn desired revenge into Christian ministry.

Having dropped out of school and trying the escape of drinking alcohol, Tatenda was fortunate enough to be drawn into a vital Anglican youth group that was active with Scripture Union, a non-denominational, Christian movement working in partnership with churches across the world since 1867. Its aim, using the Bible to inspire children, young people, and adults to know God, worked for Tatenda. He accepted Jesus Christ, moved to Harare to resume his schooling, and before long rose to leadership in this large body of young Christians. Hope was beginning to emerge out of tragedy.

At age sixteen Tatenda was in charge of this fledging church – now separated from the Anglican communion because of a dispute over the appropriateness of these young people being baptized when they already had been as infants. By age eighteen Tatenda was an evangelist holding crusades; he already had planted five new congregations, the first in 1983 under the ministry name "Eternal Word Ministries." Soon there were orphans coming to the churches. He took them into this little home and discipled them for Jesus. As they grew older, he appointed some to be pastors of his churches, all on his modest salary as a Department of Health worker.

The elders of Tatenda's churches counseled that he needed to find a wife. He knew no suitable candidates, especially anyone who would live in a tiny house filled with orphans, so he asked the elders to suggest someone. They chose a young lady who had been an evangelist and church planter herself, someone who recently sang with one of their musical groups. Lucia was a dedicated Christian worker with a wide range of talents. Tatenda had known of her, but had avoided a relationship because of her strong will and independent spirit. But now, encouraged by his elders, he made some effort to get to know her. Soon he was convinced that they were right for each other and their ministries under God.

Lucia and Tatenda Gunguwo

Tatenda and Lucia were married in 1995 and moved into a slightly larger house where there was enough space for twenty orphans, although there still was no running water. The income for the crowded household was mostly Lucia's $200 per month as a file clerk. What later would be the Dawnview Park Children's Home in Harare was in terrible shape. Even so, and without his own transportation, Tatenda continued to plant new churches and oversee their work. Sometimes he conducted as many as three "camp meetings" a year to inspire and train leaders for this growing movement. The strategy was to plant and build churches based largely on orphan ministries. It was working. The Gunguwos would have four of their own children over the next eight years, but would love and care for many more.

All of that would be in the future. First had come that providential November, 2001, airport conversation in London between Michael

141

Henderson and Lucia Gunguwo. Lucia had been excited by what she heard from Henderson about this new Horizon organization and its vision of an AIDS orphan ministry in southern Africa. Strong woman that she was, she had made her recommendation clear to Henderson:

Horizon should ask me – I prepare 75 meals a day and look after a house full of AIDS orphans, diapers and all. We grow our churches by preaching at the funerals of people who have died of AIDS. When they take the body of the victim back to their home village for burial, we go with them, preach, and plant a church. Mr. Henderson, before this friend of yours [Robert Pearson] starts more new things in South Africa for orphans, he ought to talk to a few of us practitioners who really know what it's like to care for orphaned children!

This little speech was so direct and authentic that it demanded Henderson's attention and respect. He intended to follow through with her recommendation.

Lucia Gunguwo sounded like Mother Teresa in India, bringing new life from the very beds (or back alleys) of death! Henderson would soon share this conversation with Robert Pearson when they met again in Capetown. Before leaving England, however, Henderson learned that Tatenda would be

Tatenda and Lucia Gunguwo

representing Zimbabwe at a conference in the United States in a matter of weeks. He would urge him to make special effort to meet Robert Pearson there since he also would be attending, representing Horizon International. Maybe God was in all of this. Maybe a meeting could launch a ministry partnership in Harare.

In February, 2002, with the assistance of the Billy Graham Association, Tatenda came to Washington, D.C., to attend the "Prescription for Hope" international Christian conference on HIV/AIDS. It was led by Franklin Graham and Samaritan's Purse from

February 17 to 21, 2002. About one thousand delegates were there from eighty-seven countries. Though a brand new ministry, Horizon International had been invited to participate. While there, Tatenda Gunguwo did meet Robert Pearson for the first time. In fact, one result was that arrangements were made for him to come to Indiana before returning home. He would stay with the Hendersons and meet with Horizon's board of directors on March 12. Pearson was impressed with this godly and gifted man and his selfless ministry to orphans. He could see a part of Horizon's future embedded in Tatenda's heart.

All went well at the board meeting that convened in Anderson, Indiana. Present with Robert Pearson and Tatenda Gunguwo were board members Barry Callen, Eric Dwiggins, and Jeffrey Jenness. The board had a profitable conversation and then voted enthusiastically (1) to name Tatenda and Lucia Gunguwo as Horizon's regional coordinators for the Harare/Mashonaland area of Zimbabwe, (2) to provide child sponsorships for some of the orphans living in their home, and (3) to set in place a strategic plan for building Horizon's work in the Harare area through the Gunguwos. It was the beginning of much more than could possibly have been seen in 2002.

The home of Tatenda and Lucia soon would be known by Horizon as Dawnview Park Children's Home. A hard compromise was required of the Gunguwos. They would have to remain politically neutral, learning to live with the government that had brutally killed Tatenda's father – otherwise their ministry and partnership with Horizon would be

First meeting of Tatenda Gunguwo and
Horizon's board of directors, 2002

143

impossible. They agreed and have remained apart from politics. Christian ministry to children was far more important than personal revenge.

From the Gunguwo home, it now was hoped, needy children in other parts of Harare and beyond would be able to see a new day dawning. Orphaned children would learn that there were those who would care for them, and that some White people could be trusted and even loved. That was the beginning of so much that was to follow on the Zimbabwe side of the Limpopo River.

ON TO HARARE, BULAWAYO, AND VICTORIA FALLS

Within months of Horizon entering Zimbabwe, an American congregation decided to help. The Antelope Road Christian Fellowship in Citrus Heights, California, donated $2,300 to enable the purchase of the first children's home in Harare, Zimbabwe's capital city. It was named Dawnview Park Children's Home. While "Dawnview" was the previous British name for this area of Harare, it now came to mean more. It would represent Horizon's emerging ministry in general. The name focuses attention on the "horizon," enabling desperate children to finally "view the dawn" of a new day, a new life, fresh hope for tomorrow – for themselves individually and, hopefully, for their nation as a whole.

This California congregation, pastored by Rhodes Pringle, included two people who later would be crucial members of the Horizon family. Cindy Nixon would be an intern and then key staff member in South Africa. Christopher Dancy, her Sunday school teacher, would be a member of the board of directors. This Harare home housed twenty-one sponsored orphans. When the former owner donated the money to *Jehovah Jirah Trust*, the local Horizon-related organization, it was earmarked for additional land acquisition.

Once $15,000 more was raised for remodeling the Dawnview Park Children's Home, more was envisioned. Maybe Horizon could eventually build its first extensive children's village. It could include a central facility where the project supervisor would live and the children eat and study. Surrounding it could be small "rondavals," each housing 6-8 orphans and a caregiver couple, with a total of as many as one hundred children. On the grounds could be developed a school for carpentry, welding, and sewing. Once complete, this model could be repeated elsewhere in Zimbabwe. It was only a dream waiting for resources to make it reality.

Dawnview Park Children's Home

New bunkbeds for Dawnview Park

The intent was noble and real. However, this was Zimbabwe. Any progress would be slow and very difficult. Repair work on the old house required cement that had to be trucked in from South Africa. During Horizon's first Vision Tour and work camp in February-March, 2003, the traveling team faced a soaring local inflation rate and corrupt bureaucracy that made it difficult to buy simple tools and paint. Even so, Horizon donors by now had given $12,500 to provide utilities and furnishings for the home, and the Americans were determined to accomplish all they could. Overcrowding was also a clear problem.

The Horizon visitors in early 2003 included Robert Pearson, Robert and Bonnie Powlison, Joyce Chapple, and Eric Dwiggins. While the men washed walls in preparation for painting, Bonnie and Joyce conducted a vacation Bible school as best they could in those circumstances. Eric gave a memorable dramatic performance of David and Goliath, with excited sound effects gladly provided by the children. This was a life-changing few days for the visiting Americans.

Eric Dwiggins entertaining the Dawnview Park kids

Once home in Colorado, the Powlisons made sure that the Horizon story spread in their home congregation, Creekside Church in Aurora, and in other nearby settings and events. Bonnie would join the board of directors of Horizon in January, 2006, and soon after become its treasurer. Having been with the children in Africa changes people into committed servants of the Horizon cause.

The Gunguwos were under great family pressure, trying to care for their own personal children and about thirty orphans crowded into the home. They soon were enabled to rent their own home, with Mavis Mangena and Edline Matamotara moving into Dawnview as resident caregivers paid out of child sponsorship funds. Purchased for the Gunguwos to use was a quality vehicle – transportation of people and goods was critical. Buildings and new bunk-beds were all necessary. Lucia Gunguwo proved an effective administrator. It was all about those needy but wonderful children.

The Christmas of 2003 really came for Horizon's president Robert Pearson when he again was visiting Dawnview Park and gazed into the hope-filled eyes of four-year-old Tendai Machokoto. She now had a safe home, something very new for her. The Gunguwos had found her at a bus stop, abandoned in a public place by loving parents who could no longer provide care. They were dying of AIDS. They apparently hoped that someone would come along and save her life. The someone turned out to be Horizon International, through the inspired ministry of the Gunguwos. As Pearson, his own eyes tearing up, looked into Tendai's smiling face, he saw a young lady who now knew what it was to be loved!

As Christ had come to Bethlehem to let the whole world know of God's amazing love, Horizon was coming to Zimbabwe to stand alongside the Gunguwos and others in spreading the wonderful news of Christian love, one child at a time! One of the earliest children saved from the streets and likely death was Adam Kamundi. He was one of the original Horizon orphans to be cared for at Dawnview Park Children's Home. Within a very few years under Horizon's sponsorship, Adam would do much more than survive. He would graduate from high school, become a church planter and pastor, and be on his way to higher education in medical school. In his capable hands, healing and Christian love would move to a new generation of Africans.

Adam Kamundi

Now able to devote more time to ministry supervision and expansion, the Gunguwos soon recommended that Horizon open a second orphan center in Harare. It would be Epworth Park Children's Home in the Epworth region near the international airport, likely the poorest district in Harare. There were many AIDS orphans in this community. The new home would begin with twenty to thirty children as funds allowed. This recommendation was approved by the Horizon board of directors, with the understanding that appropriate caregivers had to be found for all orphans in Epworth Park accepted by Horizon, and that the Gunguwos were to be freed to lease a separate home for themselves.

Lucia Gunguwo reported that Edline and Mavis, working wonderfully at Dawnview Park, were ready to lead separate homes. So, while Edline remained at Dawnview Park, Mavis would be given responsibility for the new home in Epworth Park. One of the housekeeping assistants would go with her and additional help would be found for each place. By the opening of 2004, the Harare Health Department formally licensed Horizon's two homes in the city, but for only twenty children each. Since both were already exceeding this number, the staffs were authorized to begin placing select children in private family homes, thus mixing the central children's home and the home-based ministry strategies.

Horizon needed some Zimbabwe-based organizational structure in order to operate legally in the country. Such a structure would provide local stability and legitimacy, and it would prove reasonable protection for the home organization in the United States. The pre-existing organization, *Jehovah Jirah Trust*, began to serve this purpose, while *Voice of Peace* was developed as the not-for-profit entity through which Horizon's child sponsorship ministry could be administered. Both of the Gunguwos were members of its board. Given the nation's political instability, it was judged wise to maintain both the former and the new organization. The wisdom of this would become evident in 2008 when the government turned against not-for-profits like *Voice of Peace*.

The ruling political party, ZANU-PF, and the country's president, Robert Mugabe, had been silencing political opposition, stressing Black empowerment, and were especially hostile to anything "Western." This government appeared to Horizon's president to be "modeling itself after pre-World War II Nazi Germany." Such a situation would be a constant challenge for Horizon, a ministry clearly based in the West, although organized and functioning in Zimbabwe on behalf of very real human needs there.

How could Horizon continue to operate when so many organizations linked to North America and Europe were downsizing or pulling out their staffs altogether from Zimbabwe? The answer would be to team with local leaders, the Gunguwos in particular, and work through *Jehovah Jirah Trust* and *Voice of Peace*, with which Horizon would partner instead of control. The government to date had not been opposing trusts, especially ones functioning with local identity and control. In this way, Horizon would remain in this troubled country, ministering legally and against difficult odds.

Robert Pearson knew well Church of God missionaries Stanley and Marion Hoffman who earlier had remained in Uganda during very difficult years of extreme violence – with wonderful ministry results. He had been inspired by their selfless example. Horizon also would stay the course in Zimbabwe, weathering the storm, saving the children, building trust, and not leaving when times were hard. Such courageous presence, however, was dangerous at times. One incident would never be forgotten.

It happened during the first Vision Tour of Horizon in the spring of 2003. Robert Pearson, Robert Powlison, and Lucia Gunguwo were on their way to the mother church facility of the Eternal Word Ministries movement. They were on the south Bulawayo highway out of Harare, having left Dawnview Park Children's Home. They were going to lead a conference on spiritual gifts, but suddenly, on a narrow road heading to the property, a large crowd of angry young adults swarmed from the tall grass. They were members of the government's youth militia, thugs recruited by the ZANU-PF party to spread intimidation and violence in areas known for supporting opposition to the government. They surrounded the van and began rocking it back and forth. They pulled open a door and began dragging Pearson out.

Lucia was very frightened, but intervened as calmly as she could. She explained that Pearson was a Christian minister, and all of them were non-political church workers. When one of the more sober youth saw the box of Spiritual Gifts Inventories and recognized the Bible references, they backed off from the intended murder, threatened the group, and finally let them go. For the remainder of their time in Harare, the Horizon group stayed in their quarters at Harare Theological College, not risking any more venturing out into the politically volatile city. Once back in the United States, Pearson read a Reuters wire story about a big White man who had been pulled from a van on the south Bulawayo road and killed. Fortunately, God remains on the throne, and the news is not always totally accurate!

A 2007 Vision Tour group of Horizon visits
the statue of David Livingstone and Victoria Falls

Opportunities for ministry in Zimbabwe quickly presented themselves well beyond the capital city of Harare – and in spite of all the social unrest. They were enabled in part by the existence of the *Jehovah Jirah Trust*, to which local officials could relate in politically delicate circumstances, and partly because of the amazing ministry of Tatenda and Lucia Gunguwo. Tatenda was functioning as bishop of a growing network of congregations that he and his leaders had planted. Horizon endeavored to expand its orphan ministries by aligning with these congregations. That had been the case with both Dawnview Park and Epworth Park in Harare. Now focus would shift to the northwest (Victoria Falls), northeast (Mt. Darwin/Chesa), and southern (Bulawayo) sections of Zimbabwe. Ministering to orphans sometimes lay at the heart of church planting and church life.

In July, 2003, Robert Pearson flew to Victoria Falls, a tourist center located on the Zambezi River. The town sits near a great waterfalls, one of the natural wonders of the world explored in the nineteenth century by David Livingstone, the famous Christian missionary. Despite the breathtaking beauty of the area, the people were troubled. Some sixty percent of the local pregnant women were infected with HIV/AIDS. Accompanied by Timothy Kumfer, an American pastor from Indiana, Pearson soon learned that the City Council of Victoria Falls was anxious to donate property for a new AIDS orphan ministry. The mayor invited him to a meeting of the Council, with the local chapter of Rotary International and the Pastors Fraternal also invited. Having heard

Gathering of the leaders of Victoria Falls

Pearson's burden for the children, an invitation was extended to Horizon International to launch a local ministry.

Pearson carried this news to Horizon's board of directors, which voted on July 24, 2003, to authorize the beginning of a Victoria Falls Strategic Ministry Center. A seven-member local board was formed and submitted to the Zimbabwean government

Robert Pearson and Mayor Dilip Pandya

for approval. At first, only two children were sponsored in Victoria Falls while local leadership was sought. But "only" was not the right word for the Tshuma family. Edson's two younger sisters were the ones sponsored – no more hunger and fear in this African home! Again, as necessary, it would be one child at a time.

The needed leadership for Horizon soon emerged in the person of Dilip Pandya, a former mayor of Victoria Falls. He was a nominal Hindu now led to belief in Jesus Christ by Horizon's president, Robert Pearson. Pandya was a gifted administrator who could launch community-wide initiatives, like he had done in establishing the city's Rotary Club. The

Sharon Parry

local board of directors of Horizon endorsed this new leadership and it was affirmed by Horizon's board of directors back in the United States on August 26, 2004. Maybe now this branch of Horizon in Zimbabwe could begin to flourish.

Unfortunately, Pandya soon resigned his leadership for health and political reasons. The City Council, however, remained supportive of Horizon and still was offering prime local property for its ministry. In 2005, Sharon Parry was appointed as Horizon's project director in Victoria Falls. She was an active member of the Victoria Falls Community Church, had been trained in orphan care, and would begin to give stability to this work. The political circumstance worsened in 2008 as the time of presidential election arrived. While Parry carried on bravely, Pandya found it necessary to leave the country, making contact with Horizon's home offices as a continuing friend of the ministry in his troubled land.

That was Victoria Falls to the northwest. In the northeast of the country was one of the many churches under the supervision of Tatenda Gunguwo. It was in the area of Mt. Darwin/Chesa. The pastor and his wife were themselves orphans who had grown up in the Gunguwo home and been mentored into Christian ministry by Tatenda. This Chesa congregation of 300 included some 160 orphans, with hundreds more barely existing in the immediate area. These 160 orphans were gathered to have their photos taken as part of applying for possible Horizon sponsorship.

On August 26, 2004, the Horizon board of directors accepted a proposed gift from the local parents' association to the Horizon-related

Tatenda Gunguwo teaching the children

So many children waiting for sponsorship

organization *Voice of Peace*. It was a local school now to be an orphan educational center. While the buildings needed considerable repair, the ministry potential was high and would proceed once circumstances were stabilized and the actual deed transfer was accomplished. This finally happened in 2009.

A fourth region of Zimbabwe also emerged for the expanding ministry of Horizon. Surprisingly, its origins rooted back to Indianapolis, Indiana. Jenny Carstens of South Africa had spoken at a women's luncheon in Indianapolis in May, 2004. A woman came forward to identify Alick and Vidah Phiri, a Zimbabwean couple who had lived in her home while attending Indiana University. This led to president Robert Pearson meeting them in Victoria Falls, Zimbabwe.

The Phiris were found to be gifted and sacrificial Christians who worked in the health-care field in Bulawayo, the second largest city in Zimbabwe. Alick was once a civil engineer, holding a masters degree in that field. Vidah, a registered nurse, was once head nurse over a staff of two hundred in a large private hospital in Bulawayo. They both were active in the Bulawayo Baptist Church, and their hearts had been drawn to an AIDS orphan ministry. Their vision and that of Horizon fit together perfectly.

Accordingly, the Horizon board of directors, on August 26, 2004, authorized the naming of the Phiris as Horizon's regional coordinators for the Bulawayo/Matebeleland region of southern Zimbabwe. Initially, they would work through the auspices of the Bulawayo Baptist Church. Alick would give half-time to building the necessary infrastructure for a new AIDS ministry.

Ray Motsi, pastor of the church who once spoke before Parliament in England, was a national Christian leader in Zimbabwe. He had been arrested in 2003 for "acts of disobedience" – protesting certain practices of the government of Zimbabwe. Despite Motsi likely being watched by the government, Horizon's Robert Pearson met him in November, 2004, and was favorably impressed. When a local board of directors for the new Horizon ministry was appointed and first met in January, 2005, there were six members, with Ray Motsi named the chair by the local group.

Cindy Nixon (DeBeer), Alick Phiri, and Samantha Morden (Frazier)

Food distribution at Mbembezi Baptist Church

155

Sponsored orphans were now coming to Horizon from the Bulawayo Baptist Church and satellite churches in Matabeleland. Registration of this new ministry was completed with the civil authorities as a Bulawayo branch of Horizon's larger ministry. Later, Ray Motsi formed his own not-for-profit organization, with Alick and Vidah Phiri then assuming the role of Horizon's ministry leaders in this part of Zimbabwe.

The first child to be sponsored in the Bulawayo area through Horizon was in November, 2005. It was an eleven-year-old girl who had never been to school. When the Phiris gave her the sponsorship news and told her that she was about to go to school, she could not contain her happiness. As Vidah Phiri later reported: "She ran around the small hut, calling out to her mother that she would finally be going to school! It is beyond my description how excited she was. When we brought her the school uniforms, she could not believe it. She kept asking us, 'Are these *my* uniforms? Is this *my* school bag?' She went on and on. This is what I tell people that Horizon can do, one child at a time."

Vidah and Alick Phiri

By 2007, however, the ministry of Horizon was facing difficult times in Zimbabwe. Unusually dry weather, a crumbling city infrastructure, a dramatic inflation rate, and political instability were troubling the nation. In Bulawayo, the Phiris were forced to scour the city for the food and fuel necessary to sustain the orphans under their care. This city of more than a million people, with surrounding dams, tree-lined streets, and stately Victorian buildings erected earlier by the British, was in deep trouble, as was the nation as a whole. Even so, the Phiris remained faithful to their high calling from God and their partnership with Horizon International.

Despite Zimbabwe's social chaos in 2008, with some 90% of the nation's school-age children not in school, every Horizon-sponsored child in Bulawayo had a school uniform, most made in a Horizon sewing center, was active in school, and advanced to the next grade level at year's end. The chaos, however, was to worsen. Soon being faced would be school closings and waves of violence. Even so, Horizon's staff would continue to serve faithfully.

Robert Pearson, Alick Phiri, Barry Callen, and Tatenda Gunguwo

BRUTALIZING THE CHILDREN!

It was unusual for a movie made in the 1950s, but most of the classic *The African Queen* was actually filmed in Africa. Even so, there apparently was an exception, even for this film. Because the Ruiki River was teeming with crocodiles, parasites, and leeches, a few scenes were shot in an indoor tank in London, England. Safety of the famous film stars was judged a paramount consideration. Unfortunately, even Christian mission organizations have been known to avoid any ministry with real risk involved. Horizon International, however, and especially its president, Robert Pearson, have left the usual pattern. They have taken significant risks in order to serve orphaned children facing death.

For Horizon, the most prominent area of risk has been Zimbabwe where Robert Mugabe has been in power since 1980. *Parade Publications* of New York identified him as 2008's number one "worst dictator" in the world. He beat out Omar al-Bashir of Sudan, Kim Jong-il of North Korea, Than Shwe of Burma (Myanmar), Sayyid Ali Khamenei of Iran, Muammar al-Qaddafi of Libya, and the others. In 2008, Zimbabwe had an unemployment rate of 85%, at least 3,800 dead from cholera, and a $50 billion note in circulation, barely enough to buy two loaves of bread. Hundreds were dead and thousands tortured and raped for threatening or potentially threatening President Mugabe's absolute rule.

Conditions in Zimbabwe have been fragile and dangerous for years, but a particularly serious political crisis erupted in 2008. It soon brought international headlines and danger to many local citizens, and to people associated with Horizon's ministry in the country. The nation's president was seeking reelection and facing growing opposition despite the intolerance for such a thing. The economy in general was reaching disasterous proportions and the population, and even neighboring countries were judging that something desperately needed to change. Key persons around Zimbabwe's president began to take drastic action to ensure that Mr. Mugabe did not lose power. Horizon's president later would refer to what happened next as "a political and economic upheaval that unleashed a tidal wave of violence." Horizon's people were caught in the middle of it, and many of them would suffer greatly.

Tatenda Gunguwo, Horizon's leader in the region of the capital city, Harare, sent a very disturbing report to Horizon's president, Robert Pearson, on May 22, 2008. He titled the lengthy and heart-wrenching email "Cry from Zimbabwe." It was fortunate that the email even got out of the country – communication was being censored carefully.

Widespread violence had broken out, reported Gunguwo. It was particularly bad in the Mt. Darwin district where Tatenda's churches and pastors apparently were being targeted by the government's youth militias and military. The orphan-care network in the area was being seriously damaged – and worse was yet to come. Sixty-eight refugees suddenly had crowded into the Gunguwo home, having fled other places with only the clothes on their backs. This number soon doubled, putting Tatenda and his wife Lucia in even greater danger from the government. While not political activists themselves, they now were helping the desperate and insisting that the church stand alongside the poor and oppressed, the hunted and terrorized in Zimbabwe. Simple humanitarianism, let alone Christian compassion, would allow no less.

It was hardly a time for cautious diplomacy; it was a time for courage and justice, especially for the children. Thinking of Robert Mugabe, Zimbabwe's president, Tatenda Gunguwo's email quoted the earlier words of Desmond Tutu of South Africa: "Mr. Minister, *you are not God.* You are merely a man. And one day your name will be only a faint scribble on the pages of history, while the name of Jesus Christ, the Lord of the church, lives forever." Tatenda was prepared to obey Jesus Christ, he wrote, "even though the human laws forbid me and suffering be the consequence." Sudden death was also a clear possibility. The email asked that Horizon people in the United States be called to prayer and stand as faithful partners with their brothers and sisters in Zimbabwe.

Robert Pearson was a spiritual mentor to Tatenda Gunguwo and his whole network of pastors in Zimbabwe. He earlier had encouraged these pastors to stand for justice if and when circumstances became dire. The circumstances now were dire, and the pastors and Gunguwo, their prophetic church leader, were taking their stand. Pearson felt morally obligated to these pastors and went into action. He contacted Horizon's corporate secretary, Barry Callen, initiating a sober discussion between them about what response to make to the shocking report and heartfelt plea. Soon an emergency letter of appeal for prayer and funds was sent out to Horizon's child sponsors and other donors and friends across North America. Food needed to be bought in quantity and somehow delivered to increasingly desperate Zimbabwean orphans in Horizon's care.

Tatenda Gunguwo displaying food from the parched earth

A hastily arranged trip to South Africa was soon made by Pearson, taking emergency money with him and meeting with Horizon partners on the ground in South Africa. Planning was done for the delivery of aid – a complicated and dangerous business that was nonetheless necessary. Horizon board member Christopher Dancy happened to be in South Africa at the time and joined the intervention team. The donor base back in the United States had responded to the emergency appeal with an amazing $84,000! This was used in July, August, and September of 2008, primarily for the purchase and delivery of emergency food and other supplies to Zimbabwe. Some of the money was retained for the time when the violence quieted and it was determined how best to help rebuild the shattered lives of children, their care-givers, and the supporting churches and pastors. How this was all done was not disclosed to protect the brave people involved.

Reported Tatenda Gunguwo at Horizon's African Team Retreat convened in Zambia in October, 2008: "When word got to Bob Pearson, he immediately came to South Africa without regarding his own safety. I met him and Christopher Dancy there and we had to restrain him from crossing into Zimbabwe where he would be in great danger. We felt that we had a man who is our family member, one who will stand with us in any situation." Jesus had gone to the cross, doing the will of the Father. Horizon expressed a similar love, also doing the Father's will.

The emerging story of what had happened in Zimbabwe was gruesome. Churches had been forcibly closed for a time. Many congregational leaders had been taken to "re-education" camps where they were beaten and strongly urged to denounce the opposition political party. The Chesa Children's Home had been claimed for a time by the local government youth militia for its Mt. Darwin district headquarters. The young orphan girls living there were brutally and repeatedly raped. Back in Harare, the capital, a few of Horizon's sponsored children were actually killed in Epworth Park, with a large section of this impoverished community burned to the ground. Some fifteen of Horizon's orphan care-givers and volunteers were murdered for suspected political activity, including even the perception of an inclination to vote against the country's president.

Two stories will suffice to show the horror of the circumstance. The first involves four Horizon orphan caregivers, all elderly grandmothers. They were arrested and brought to Harare by a government youth militia. They were held, with their legs and arms outstretched, and repeatedly thrown into the air. Each time they were thrown up, they were allowed to drop to the ground, brutally breaking bones. All of them finally died on the spot. The watching crowd was told, "If you vote for the Movement for Democratic Change, this will happen to you!"

The second story involves a seven-year-old boy. He was taken into the Borrowdale Children's Home during 2008, the property in Harare then also serving as the home of the Gunguwos and, for a time, nearly seventy refugees fleeing the violence. Each morning this boy would waken himself with his uncontrolled crying. He thought that his mother was calling him to report that his brothers and sisters had all just died in the turmoil! In fact, his parents were already dead and his surviving siblings had been scattered to various people who would take them in. What soon became clear was that this little boy, during the presidential re-election chaos, had witnessed the militias killing people. It was haunting him. Horizon was now his only family, his only hope.

Sandra Zinyama

There were numerous such stories, unfortunately. By God's grace, however, there also soon emerged a few more positive things. For instance, in the fall of 2009, soon after their wedding, Robert and Christine Pearson traveled to Zimbabwe, part of their "celebration tour" during which local ministry leaders and others joined in their personal joy. It was still not a comfortable place, but it now was time to return and emphasize the good. The Pearsons encountered Sandra Zinyama while in Mt. Darwin. She was a nine-year-old orphan, had been reported missing during the earlier violence, and had been raped. The Gunguwos arranged for her to be taken to Borrowdale, the ministry center of the

Gunguwos in Harare, where she could be cared for properly. The recovery would be slow, but sure, like the food that was being grown in parched ground in various Horizon ministry sites.

Finally, with President Mugabe claiming that he had been successfully reelected, it was hoped that relative calm would begin to return to the nation. The essentially sham reelection was to include a power sharing with the opposition party, but the atmosphere remained toxic and dangerous. Mugabe continued to resist any real power sharing, and to blame western countries for the tremendous problems in his country. A few of Horizon's sponsored chil-

Robert and Christine Pearson now sponsor Sandra Zinyama

dren in Harare died of cholera – bad water nearly everywhere and virtually no medicine in the country. The common note of currency was

The dramatically inflated currency of Zimbabwe

100 billion dollars (soon to grow into the trillions!) – signaling that the economy had basically collapsed. Schools were closed across the nation for a long period of time.

Horizon was determined to lead the way to some healing and resumed ministry, despite the costs and risks. Plans were made to send a team of American pastors and counselors into the country to conduct a pastor's conference for 135 Shona pastors of churches under the supervision of Horizon's ministry partners, Tatenda and Lucia Gunguwo. They were facilitating Horizon's orphan-care ministry in eastern Zimbabwe where about 450 children were being sponsored, and where there was a waiting list of over 6,000 more orphans! Faithfulness to a compassionate God left no choice but to accept the risks.

The theme of the February, 2009, pastor's conference was "Rebuilding the Walls of Ministry in Zimbabwe." A ministry of Horizon "presence" was crucial in a setting where it had been dangerous for Americans to even be seen. Skilled and loving care-givers were needed to minister to traumatized children and tortured adults who had suffered confinement in "re-education" camps. There now were many new HIV+ women who needed information, guidance, and support – many had been raped and contracted the dreaded disease during the time of social chaos and desperation. Horizon would continue to stand alongside the persecuted.

Like in the biblical book of Nehemiah, on which the conference was based, those who had suffered in exile were back home – at least those who had survived. There had been much destruction of life and property. Now it was time to "rebuild the walls of Jerusalem" (Neh. 2:17). God had not abandoned Zimbabwe or its people, exile or not.

The conference, convened in Harare and hosted by Tatenda and Lucia Gunguwo, ministered to church leaders deeply scarred by the violence that had marked the Zimbabwean presidential and parliamentary elections of March through July, 2008. Members of the visiting Horizon team washed the feet of the Gunguwos as a public act of humble partnership in the compassionate ministry of Jesus Christ. The prophetic voice of Tatenda announced: "The bottle of tears is now full. We have wept enough. No more is needed. It is time to smile and rejoice!"

There was more. God's prophetic spokesperson quoted Zechariah

9:12 where God promises to both restore and expand his faithful people. Tatenda called on the pastors to plant ninety new churches in the year ahead. They said "yes!" Such dramatic growth was not mere rhetoric. After all, Tatenda and his leadership team already had planted 193 churches in the seven years that his Eternal Word Ministries had been

Tatenda Gunguwo blessing pastors

partners with Horizon. These inspired pastors, wounded and persecuted or not, would keep surviving and growing – and going on their new bicycles now given to them as gifts by Horizon.

As partners of Horizon, the pastors promised to heed the call and trust God for the harvest. The new churches would be places where orphans could be fed, educated, filled with God's love, and nurtured to be future leaders with character and vision. How could the pastors, so persecuted themselves, manage to launch all these new churches? They would use the social crisis all around them as the building blocks of tomorrow. They would begin Bible clubs for orphans, wash the clothes of widows, teach women how to be midwives (most of the hospitals were closed), and set up support groups for HIV-positive women. In short,

New bicycles for increased ministry

they would gather the hurting to places where they would be loved in practical ways. They would wash them in the love of Jesus. New churches would be born and orphans would be in families again!

There was another dimension to this February, 2009, pastor's conference. The women of the visiting American team were asked to go to Epworth Park and speak to a new women's support group. This community had been one of the hardest hit by the recent political turmoil, with many women of all ages raped – and others turning to prostitution as the only way they knew to feed their children. Horizon was sponsoring 166 children in this community, with several killed or missing in the turmoil. There soon were signs of a *spiritual revival* breaking out from the very ashes of the violence and human misery.

Lucia Gunguwo had started a women's ministry in Epworth Park, Harare, in January, 2009, partly by distributing food that had arrived in a container sent by Horizon. Tatenda came to preach. During the February pastor's conference, Deborah Bergstrom, a pastor's wife from Houston, Texas, spoke there to fifty women on the subject "Turning Bitterness into Forgiveness." She and Kimberly Richardson, now a seminary student in southern California, returned the next day to find 312 women present, with fifteen committing their lives to Jesus Christ. Only weeks later, the Gunguwos were in Epworth Park leading Christian worship, with an estimated 2,500 people standing in the rain to hear good news! Many repented of whatever they had done, or expressed forgiveness for whatever had been done to them.

A revival had caught fire, cleansing lives and lighting the way to a new future. Soon, other Horizon groups from the United States would come to this area to continue this amazing ministry opportunity. One

Children in Epworth Park, Harare, Zimbabwe

group led a women's convention attended by 4,500 women! A group from the Pendleton Christian Church of Pendleton, Indiana, conducted a large Bible school for Epworth Park children.

Many young couples were living together in Epworth Park and couldn't afford weddings. The Gunguwos began couples' meetings to strengthen families, at one point encouraging them to participate in a mass wedding ceremony. Twenty-three couples responded, with Lucia providing wedding gowns and tuxedos for them all, and with national newspapers in Zimbabwe covering the unusual event. Women who had been supporting their children by prostitution were given loans to get off the streets and begin legitimate businesses.

Tatenda Gunguwo was brought to the United States in May-June, 2009, to speak in a series of Horizon settings, telling the story, giving thanks, and encouraging additional support for his troubled homeland. American hearts and wallets opened. Yes, Horizon had crossed the Limpopo River and joined God in spreading love and hope in Zimbabwe. Once back home, Tatenda wrote to Horizon's president Pearson about the crossroads now being faced by his homeland:

> *Politics has failed. The whole infrastructure has broken down – health, industry, finance, education, engineering, mining, farming, and so on. The government is broken and confused. The new unity government is non-functional. The government is currently drafting a new constitution, and the church has been invited to participate in the process.*

After quoting Tatenda's observation in an August, 2009, newsletter, Pearson said to the many North American churches and individuals supporting Horizon's ministry: "I am personally haunted by a question: Will the church respond and provide leadership out of the morass? Or will the church turn away?" No matter what the morass has been or yet will be, Horizon was determined to *never turn away!*

Jennifer Rottinghaus

Chapter Seven

FORWARD TO UGANDA, ZAMBIA, KENYA

The mission of Horizon International focuses on Africa, with its ministry beginning originally in South Africa. Soon, however, it became obvious that God had much more in mind for this ministry. Zimbabwe surged into view and new ministries were launched northward across the Limpopo River. For Horizon, the mission then continued to expand into Uganda, Zambia, and soon Kenya. The human disaster resulting from the HIV/AIDS pandemic was that widespread. God's heart was broken for all who suffered, and the calls for help kept coming to Horizon.

Horizon's leaders were faced with a struggle. How much ministry expansion should be attempted, given limited staff, financial resources, and administrative support. Even with the limitations, decisions were made to keep reaching out in faith. God kept providing what is required – and that was much! The advance into new countries required more and more ministry partners – congregations, individuals, foundations, and governments. This need has been divinely supplied, and often in surprising and deeply gratifying ways.

The goal has never been to build Horizon International for its own sake. It has been to keep strengthening this ministry in order to better serve the great needs of more and more AIDS orphans, and in more and more ways and places. God obviously has been at work. Expansion has come as doors have opened, often with clear evidence of divine direction. The staff of Horizon has grown, as have the number of orphans being served, and even the number of African countries whose borders the Horizon ministry has found itself crossing. Disease does not respect national boundaries. Suffering, especially of helpless children, is tragic wherever it exists.

Extensive ministry expansion was being urged by some people on both sides of the Atlantic Ocean. Even so, such expansion was judged by the board of directors to be premature, not yet God-directed. For example, a call came from India, asking Horizon to consider crossing continents! A major leader of the Church of God in India, Borman Roy Sohkhia, made the request. He hoped that Horizon would launch work in his nation since the projection was that AIDS would be spreading rapidly on that sub-continent in the years immediately ahead.

Painfully, this call from India was declined by Horizon's board of directors in its January 30, 2004, meeting. This decision was based on three reasons. The staff and resources of Horizon were judged inadequate for such expansion, the mission statement of Horizon would need to be altered to encompass such a major geographic shift, and, since there was so very much still to do in southern and eastern Africa, it appeared premature to make such a mission alteration.

Horizon International had begun its ministry outreach in South Africa. Soon the ministry had come to include the nations of Zimbabwe, Uganda, and Zambia, with Kenya likely to be next. One could see that God was graciously building the Horizon ministry in a paced and focused manner. God was opening new ministry opportunities, helping it discover new resources for doing the ever-enlarging task, and stimulating the creativity and relationships necessary to establish and use multiple ways of proceeding on multiplying fronts. Consult chapter eight for an overview of various ministry means Horizon was coming to employ. They were different, yes, but all were conceived and implemented in the service of Horizon's primary mission, the serving of AIDS orphans.

Reaching Uganda

The story of Horizon's beginnings in South Africa and then Zimbabwe are found in earlier chapters. The next nation to be entered by Horizon was Uganda. With Kampala its capital city, Uganda is a landlocked country in East Africa, bordered by Kenya, Sudan, the Democratic Republic of the Congo, Rwanda, and Tanzania. It achieved independence from the United Kingdom in 1962.

The 1970s and 1980s were deeply troubled decades for Uganda under the dictatorial regimes of Idi Amin and Milton Obote. There were at least 300,000 deaths resulting from government action in Uganda and the nearby fighting in the Democratic Republic of the Congo. Welcome democratic reforms have come in more recent years. The human rights practices and national economy of Uganda have improved considerably. Yoweri Museveni has been in power since 1986 and has been lauded by the West as part of a welcome new generation of African leaders.

The Rev. Silas Atugonza first met Horizon's president Robert Pearson at the June, 2000, North American Convention of the Church of God convened in Anderson, Indiana. It was there that Pearson introduced Atugonza to that church's General Assembly as an honored international guest. By early 2005 this significant Ugandan church leader had followed up on this relationship. He had written to Pearson to ask for help, knowing that in the meantime Pearson had established the new Horizon ministry. After being informed of this correspondence and new ministry possibility, Horizon's board of directors encouraged Pearson to visit Uganda to explore possible Horizon expansion in that land.

One of the reasons for this exploration of potential expansion was that Horizon's board of directors had interest in Horizon joining a consortium of small Christian organizations that were going to solicit funds from USAID. A requirement, however, was that a candidate organization must be at work in at least two countries recognized by the State Department of the United States (and the troubled nation of Zimbabwe was not so recognized).

Silas and Betty Atugonza oversee a group of about two hundred congregations called the "Eternal Church of God." These churches are

Silas and Betty Atugonza

located mostly in the Fort Portal area of western Uganda, with some spilling over into neighboring Rwanda and the Democratic Republic of the Congo. Fort Portal is a lovely location, situated at about 5,000 feet altitude, overlooking mountains and volcanoes, with tea estates and a forest nearby.

This region of Uganda is sometimes called the "land of enchantment," the place to which tourists flock to see the mountain gorillas. Robert Pearson arrived in Fort Portal in early March, 2005, accompanied by Diane and Michael Carey. They had not come to see gorillas, but to witness firsthand the great need of the children. The Atugonzas already had mobilized their churches to document the AIDS orphans in their communities – some 10,000 children had been identified!

Since no European or North American child sponsor organization had yet come to minister in the Fort Portal area, Horizon's arrival was cause for local celebration. The visiting Americans were greeted by a

A Horizon partner church in Fort Poral, Uganda

local band and enjoyed worship services in several settings, including the Rwengoma Eternal Church of God where 3,300 people greeted the visiting Americans (there were 1,500 orphans among them!).

Soon files were opened and photographs taken of numerous children being screened for possible Horizon sponsorship. Various local ministries already were being administered effectively by the Atugonzas and others, but the problems still being faced were substantial to say the least – according to one estimate, nearly 45% of the people in this region of Uganda were living with HIV/AIDS! Even though Uganda's national government had been working vigorously and quite successfully against the further spread of HIV/AIDS, infection rates remained alarmingly high in the Fort Portal region.

One key reason for this continuing high infection rate was rebel activities in recent years. Such violence had kept aid organizations and government assistance to a minimum. While the area had now become relatively secure, thousands of AIDS orphans still existed, were in great need, and anxiously waited for someone to help. By God's guidance and provision, that someone would be Horizon International.

Robert Pearson soon reported to Horizon's board of directors his "amazement" at the quality of ministry work already being done under the supervision of the Atugonzas. He went on to report his pleasure that these Ugandan leaders, so aware of how much more ministry was needed, were anxious to partner with Horizon. Therefore, Pearson recommended to the board that Horizon begin a partnership ministry in Fort Portal, Uganda. The Atugonzas were

Photos of children being taken by Diane Carey in Uganda, 2005

named regional coordinators for Horizon and would proceed to register Horizon as a new domestic not-for-profit organization in Uganda. The board of directors, on March 24, 2005, approved this new Horizon beginning, believing that God's hand was in it.

By December, 2005, Horizon already had under full sponsorship thirty-six Ugandan orphans, with hundreds of others fully screened and ready when North American sponsors could be found. The Atugonzas already were functioning well as Horizon coordinators. They had organized their pastors and congregations into zones and established an impressive network of volunteers. These pastors, while deeply committed, were in great need of training. It was obvious that quality care of orphans needed to include the nurturing of these pastors.

Accordingly, in November, 2007, Horizon staged a major pastor's conference using a new curriculum designed by Todd Faulkner especially for the Ugandan pastors. It was anticipated that some 2,000 African pastors would attend what undoubtedly was the most extensive undertaking in Horizon's history. Partnering with Horizon in this particular effort was the ministry organization *Heart of Africa*, founded by Horizon's longtime friend Michael Henderson. A primary goal of this pastor's conference was to equip these Christian leaders, many of whom were directly responsible for the spiritual nurture of the congregations where Horizon's sponsored children were attending.

An urgent need for effective support of the orphan ministry was transportation for the pastors, especially for supervising and resourcing the orphan caregivers living in remote villages. Horizon began to raise funds back in the United States for purchasing thirty new bicycles. They soon were secured and presented to some of these Christian pastors. They were thrilled at their new mobility – and thus the means of expanding their ministries. The next year a motorcycle was purchased for the microfinance loan officer serving with *Horizon Uganda*.

Another need in the Fort Portal community was productive employment. Caregivers could serve effectively only if they could support themselves and stabilize their living circumstances. This basic need brought Horizon's first entry into the arena of microfinance (see more detail in chapter eight). This type of ministry, a means of

Proud pastors ready to ride for Jesus and
serve "the least" of God's dear children

encouraging true community transformation, centers in the establishment and administration of a revolving loan fund. These loans enable the creation of new jobs and business ventures. The resulting income serves local people and needs directly.

The first major loan proposed was for the launching of a maize mill project to employ some eighteen persons full-time. The maize produced would help feed thousands of orphans who were waiting to be sponsored through Horizon. When the loan was paid back, the money would be recycled to one or more new ventures. While an expected donor for this particular project did not materialize, numerous other projects of various kinds did emerge and were funded.

Particularly in view next was a possible dairy farm that one day would include an orphan's home, staff quarters and offices, a church, and a medical clinic. Land for this future project already had been secured. A few cows were purchased, branded, and kept on the property of the Atugonzas. It was the beginning of a herd that, it was hoped, eventually would be a full dairy farm. Nothing would be easy, but the vision was clear and a beginning had been made. Refer to chapter eight for sample success stories of the microfinance ministry – like Irene's Boutique.

Unfortunately, political trouble has not ended in and around Uganda. A long battle against an extremist rebel group in the north,

Silas Atugonza, lover of orphaned children

backed by the country of Sudan, had seen thousands of Ugandan children abducted for the purpose of being trained as rebel soldiers. This nightmare had been compounded by the HIV/AIDS pandemic that had hit this young nation, just like it has its neighbors. The disease is particularly devastating in the refugee camps along the Ugandan border. The Ugandan army had intervened in Rwanda when the Hutus were massacring the Tutsis, driving the most radical of the Hutus into the eastern Congo near the Ugandan border. The United Nations had worked to stabilize this area. In the meantime, and with few humanitarian organizations active because of the danger, the Atugonzas had been busy planting churches. Horizon International had now partnered with this pioneering ministry and currently sponsors children in Congolese refugee camps inside Uganda.

A Congolese refugee camp

By 2008, Horizon had become active in another city in Uganda far from Fort Portal. Holly Mizell had grown up in the Highland Park Community Church in Casper, Wyoming, and traveled to Uganda with a mission organization. While there, she had developed a burden for an orphan ministry. Later, she was present in Casper for a concert of the Kuyasa Kids Children's Choir. Further inspired by the work of Horizon, she returned to Uganda to launch in Jinja the "Our Own Children's Home" ministry for HIV+ children. She married a local Ugandan, William Pheni, and they began ministering together.

The "Our Own Children's Home" in Jinja, Uganda

When Robert Pearson visited this work, he was accompanied by Silas and Betty Atugonza, Horizon's regional leaders in Uganda. With very limited resources, the Phenis already were caring effectively for thirty-eight children, and expressing strong interest in expansion of their efforts. A partnership between Horizon and Holly and William Pheni was recommended by president Pearson to Horizon's board of directors in September, 2008. It was approved for immediate implementation, with the Phenis identified as Horizon's project directors. Regular support for them and their orphans has come from the Casper congregation in Wyoming, home of Holly.

William and Holly Pheni

This Jinja ministry would be Horizon's first to focus on HIV+ orphaned children, but it would not be the last. The Atugonzas were inspired with this ministry – HIV+ children are the least likely to be helped by anyone. They returned to their home in Fort Portal, Uganda, determined to begin their own such ministry. The result was the new Ibonde Children's Home.

The several Horizon ministries in Uganda were now being administered under the organizational umbrella called *Horizon Uganda*. It was registered officially with the Ugandan government and its offices were housed in a good facility in Fort Portal.

INTO ZAMBIA

The Republic of Zambia is another landlocked country in southern Africa. Lusaka, its capital city, is located in the southeast of the country. The population is concentrated mainly around Lusaka and the copperbelt to the northwest – the nation's economy has been dominated by copper mining. During the 1970s this nation began sliding into poverty and now is one of the poorest countries in the world. Previously known as Northern Rhodesia, it became the Republic of Zambia in 1964. Officially, it is a Christian country, but one with a wide range of religious thought that often is blended with Christian belief by many church groups. People make and sell whatever they can.

While Robert Pearson and Horizon's first Vision Tour group were in Stellenbosch and Kayamandi, Western Cape Province, South Africa, in February and March, 2003, Pearson had been approached by Japhet Ndhlovu, General Secretary of the Christian Council of Churches for the country of Zambia. He wanted Pearson and Cassie and Jenny Carstens to

*A typical Zambian marketplace
ready for tourists*

visit Zambia to explore AIDS ministry opportunities there. They were open to this possibility, but it would be another three years before such a visit would take place. Regardless of the delay, the visit would happen, and would lead to excellent ministry results.

Ansie Joubert was an independent Dutch Reformed missionary from South Africa with a calling from God to work in community development, particularly with women and children at risk. She knew of the AIDS work of Jenny Carstens and spent a day at Horizon's 2005 African Team Retreat. Joubert and her staff then began praying about joining the Horizon ministry team. With the encouragement of Horizon's board of directors, Robert Pearson flew to Lusaka, Zambia, in July, 2006, to explore expansion possibilities in this relatively stable country, politically speaking – especially when compared to Zimbabwe, its deeply troubled neighbor. Beneath the relative social stability, however, was the scourge of severe poverty. About two-thirds of the 12 million people were surviving on less than a dollar a day, and living with the harsh fact that over 700,000 children were already orphaned by AIDS.

Pearson was met at the Lusaka airport by Joubert. They soon stopped for a visit at Joubert's little Ministry Prayer Room housed in a shack community outside Lusaka. As this exploratory visit began, Pearson was praying, "Lord, give me discernment about a possible relationship of Horizon with Joubert and her ministry team in Zambia." Then something happened that brought a sense of this prayer's answer.

Hanging on the wall was a notice calling for prayer. It immediately captured the surprised attention of Pearson because it included a photo of Christopher Galada. Chris was a young man from South Africa well known to Pearson. Joubert had not known Chris or that he was a member of the Horizon team preparing for full-time ministry as a mentor/pastor to hearing impaired AIDS-orphaned students who attend a Horizon partner organization in South Africa, Noluthando School for the Deaf. She had received the notice and photo only because her own mother was deaf. This Galada "coincidence" was so unexpected and unlikely that it helped to convince Pearson that God was preparing a new ministry partnership for Horizon in Zambia.

Ansie Joubert

Ansie Joubert would be an excellent regional coordinator for Horizon. She would be joined shortly by other local leaders who would emerge to assist with this new work now being envisioned. Prominent among them would be a 2005 graduate of the African Leadership Institute for Community Transformation in South Africa, another ministry partner of Horizon. Mercy Dube returned to Zambia after her graduation with a burning desire to minister to orphans. She began an

Samantha Frazier, Christopher Galada, and Ina Calitz

Afternoon Children's Club as part of the expanding ministry of her home congregation, the Chongwe Pentecostal Holiness Church. Being young and still single, Dube was placed by Horizon under the supervision of the veteran missionary, Ansie Joubert, now functioning as Horizon's regional coordinator in Zambia. Dube would be a project director, beginning with the outreach ministry of her own home church.

Mercy (Dube) Banda leading orphans in a joyous song in Chongwe

Soon joining Dube as a Horizon co-worker was Derrick Banda, also a member of the Chongwe Church and a graduate of the International Sports Leadership School started by Cassie Carstens in South Africa. Banda and Dube quickly proved to be excellent project directors under Joubert's supervision. Later, they married and together they have launched new Afternoon Children's Clubs as part of the ministries of several local congregations. Horizon donors provided a truck for the delivery of food parcels to the widely scattered homes where the Horizon-sponsored children live. Their enthusiasm and creativity have been superb. It is a treat for visiting Americans to watch and listen to Mercy (Dube) Banda lead a group of orphans in a time of singing. Under her guidance, a collection of kids become an electrified choir exuding energy and joy.

The story of the lives and ministries of the Bandas is a tale of God's special grace and gifting. Kyle and Mary Beth Jackson were living in South

Africa for a few months in 2005, hosting Robert Pearson on one of his many trips there. Mary Beth had met Mercy, herself an orphan with a heart for orphan ministry. She encouraged her to meet Jenny Carstens and get acquainted with the exceptional new work of Horizon International. The Jacksons had known of Horizon since its very beginning. They had been in South Africa in 2001 on their

Derrick and Mercy (Dube) Banda

honeymoon trip, the very time when Pearson first visited Africa with Kyle's parents, Ethan and Joyce Jackson.

As time passed, Kyle and Mary Beth had become acquainted with Horizon's growing work in both the Western Cape and Limpopo provinces of South Africa and had been impressed with the exceptional quality of people Pearson had surrounded himself with in Africa. They were happy to send outstanding young African leaders Horizon's way when they could. They had such an opportunity in the case of Mercy Dube.

The personal background of Mercy Dube is a moving story of God at work. When her mother died of AIDS, this young orphan wanted nothing more to do with the God who had not answered the urgent prayers for the healing of her mother. Mercy avoided life on the streets only through the caring of some relatives and friends – agents for the mercy of God. Beginning in 2004, she found her way onto the staff of *Sport for Christ Action Zambia* and, quite naturally, was attracted especially to the great needs of orphans.

Derrick Banda was also active in *Sport for Christ Action Zambia* and then received important training at the International Sports Leadership School led by Cassie Carstens in South Africa. He also would then return to Zambia to engage in ministry in the Chongwe District. Eventually he would marry Mercy Dube. Aware of these special young leaders, Pearson was back in the United States in August, 2006, recommending to

Horizon's board of directors that it approve Horizon's immediate expansion into Zambia, including approval of the excellent leadership already in place there (Joubert, Dube, and Banda). God's hand was seen and the go-ahead was granted readily.

The initial ministry location would be in the town of Chongwe, forty-five kilometers from Lusaka, where a Pentecostal Holiness Church could provide support to sponsored orphans. Already functioning on those church grounds, under the direction of Dube and Banda, was a Children's Club involving sixty-three orphans in regular singing, games, and Bible learning. The club would become the model for similar ministries in many other locations. Soon a partner church in the United States, the Northeast Community Church in Fishers, Indiana, would develop a special support relationship with Chongwe. See page 187 for detail on this and other congregations in the United States that were choosing to partner with particular African ministry locations.

In 2007 Horizon launched an orphan ministry in Chaisa Compound in Lusaka, the capital city of Zambia. The orphans sponsored there were enrolled in a local elementary school that was renting its facility. Since actually owning the property would free up precious resources for better staffing and equipping the school, and thus provide a much higher quality of education, Horizon considered enabling a purchase. The amount of money needed was featured in Horizon's 2007 Christmas catalog. The result was not as expected. After all, each ministry launch is something of an experiment, an act of faith, a venture to be evaluated as things actually develop. In this case, developments changed the direction of things.

While some funding was successfully raised, allowing the possibility of the purchase, this school property was, in fact, not purchased by Horizon. The local pastor who was operating the school had begun acting in ways that caused Horizon to question and then end the relationship. The funds were transferred to the process of officially registering Horizon with the Zambian government. This legal recognition, under the name *Horizon Zambia*, would position Horizon well for what was soon to come, the opening of other ministries within Zambia. They would be launched and proceed in concert with quality ministry partners who would prove more compatible with Horizon's mission and ministry strategies.

The Horizon ministry continued in Chaisa Compound, with thirty-seven children sponsored by the summer of 2009. With new leadership needed, God graciously provided Joshua and Jessie Sachipita. He previously served with Zambia's organization associated with Inter-Varsity Fellowship, seeking to reach for Christ students enrolled in Lusaka universities. Jessie came to Lusaka from Zambia's northern Copper Belt. There she met and married Joshua before they joined Horizon's staff as project directors in Chaisa Compound in Lusaka.

Jessie and Joshua Sachipita

The question of determining Zambian ministry partners for Horizon brought a strategic question to the board of directors back in the United States. Should the projected new ministries proceed in relation to geographic regions of the country or through particular denominational bodies ready to partner with Horizon? Strong denominational church networks already existed and were expressing interest in such partnerships. These existing networks were adopted by the board of directors as the preferred Horizon strategy, at least in Zambia. They included the Pentecostal Holiness Church (Chongwe District), the Assemblies of God (Chaisa Compound in Lusaka), and the Church of God (Anderson) (initially in the city of Livingston).

All three church bodies were anxious for Horizon to convene pastor's conferences as a way of nurturing their leaders and introducing Horizon's orphan sponsorship program. Pearson had preached earlier at a Pentecostal Holiness congregation in Chongwe and an orphan ministry had begun there. Within two years that congregation had grown dramatically, primarily because of its orphan ministry. Word had spread that such orphan-related church growth could be the case in other locations, greatly benefitting the churches and the orphans. Several congregations now have actually experienced this growth.

Horizon and Church of God leaders in Zambia.
L. to R.: Stanley Hoffman, Robert Pearson, Mailesi Ndao, and Barry Callen

During Horizon's Vision Tour of late 2007, there were preliminary discussions with leaders of the Church of God in Zambia – associated with the Church of God (Anderson) in the United States. Included were Mailesi Ndao and veteran Canadian missionaries Stanley and Marion Hoffman, then based in Livingston, Zambia. It was clear that relationships were deepening and future partnership ministries likely would emerge.

During the summer of 2009, Ansie Joubert concluded her valuable ministry with Horizon as a regional coordinator. Fortunately, quality new leadership was immediately available. The board of directors of Horizon named Moses and Cecilia Sakala as the new Regional Coordinators for Zambia.

Moses and Cecilia Sakala

Ministry partnerships were strengthening, African leadership was functioning well, and the future of Horizon's ministries appeared bright.

ON TO KENYA

The interest of Horizon International in beginning a ministry to orphans in the country of Kenya had existed for several years. This was partly because of various contacts of president Pearson in this country, its proximity to work already begun in Jinja, Uganda, and the missionary parents of Horizon's office manager, Samantha Frazier, who are serving in Kenya. But only in 2009 did something specific develop that would trigger an actual plan for launching Horizon in Kenya.

The decision for direct exploration of a ministry launch in Kenya, East Africa, began with an action of Anderson University School of Theology in Anderson, Indiana. This seminary brought to campus for the 2008-2009 school year Dr. Robert Lang'at. He would serve as the Harp Professor-in-Residence. A casual acquaintance developed between him and Dr. Barry Callen, former dean of that seminary and Horizon's corporate secretary. This led to serious conversation in May, 2009, involving these two men, Gladys, wife of Robert, and Robert Pearson,

Horizon's president. Dr. Lang'at at the time was a lecturer and deputy principal of Highlands Bible College in Kericho, Kenya, and a minister in the African Gospel Church. His wife was an experienced public school teacher in Kericho with an evolving passion for orphan ministry.

Robert and Gladys Lang'at

Pearson and Callen were impressed by this Kenyan couple who had many credentials and numerous contacts in the educational and church communities of Kericho. Lang'at delivered two public lectures at Anderson School of Theology making clear the depth and compatibility of his vision of Christian ministry with that of Horizon's. The lectures were titled "A Biblical Theology of the Poor" and "Leadership and Working Within Cultures Not Our Own." It was noted that Horizon recently had partnered with a work in Jinja, Uganda, not that far from Kericho. President Pearson decided to recommend to the board of directors of Horizon, in its May, 2009, meeting, that the board authorize him and Barry Callen to visit Kericho when the Lang'ats would be back home and have further explored the particulars of the possible ministry launch. If all appeared in order on this visit, the ministry could begin. This pivotal visit was scheduled for July, 2010.

NEW CONGREGATIONAL ALLIES

Growing out of all of this multi-national expansion, and given the results of consultation with Horizon's ministry partners at the African Team Retreat convened in Lusaka, Zambia, in November, 2008, Horizon's board of directors acted. It approved the eventual calling of an "African Coordinator" to serve as a liaison between Horizon's home offices in the United States and all of the present and emerging African partners in the several nations where Horizon is at work. This would be implemented when an appropriate person was identified and the necessary funding became available.

Meanwhile, support for present and future ministries was coming from a widening circle of congregations in North America. Each was catching the vision and wanting to partner with Horizon International. Often these congregations became involved through personal contact, usually members of the churches and their leadership staffs traveling to Africa with Horizon and then returning with excitement and a deep burden for the great need and opportunity to serve. Sometimes they would focus on the ministry area visited, channeling their support there in multiple ways – additional trips, child sponsorships, and special project giving.

What now has emerged is a network of church allies for Horizon's mission. These allies have formed partnership packages that express a deep and committed identification with and caring for particular ministries and locations in Africa. Over time, their growing joy of accomplishment in God's service has drawn more and more people into the partnerships.

There now are many partner packages, and many aspects of the service of each. The following are a few examples of such congregations, with only brief glimpses at their ministry involvements through Horizon International.

Antelope Road Christian Fellowship, Citrus Heights, California, N. Rhodes Pringle, pastor. This has been one of the premier partner congregations of Horizon since virtually the beginning of Horizon's existence in 2001. Several of its many ministry involvements in Africa are noted elsewhere in this book.

Church of God of Exeter, Exeter, California, Wayne Putman, pastor. In May, 2009, president Pearson shared a wonderful weekend with this congregation. It decided to become very active with Horizon in multiple ways, including a serious and longterm commitment to a particular ministry area. The Mt. Darwin area of Zimbabwe was chosen. Periodic trips and regular giving were planned over the coming years.

Family Bible Church, Marshall, Michigan, Richard Gerten, pastor. This independent congregation has partnered with Horizon in Matipane Village in Limpopo Province, South Africa. These Christians purchased the equipment for the sewing center and provided food supplements for children there.

First Church of God, Alma, Michigan, Steven D. Wimmer, pastor. This congregation has committed itself especially to the expanding microfinance ministry of Horizon in Uganda. See detail in chapter eight.

Highland Park Community Church, Casper, Wyoming, John L. Spear, pastor. This congregation has focused helpfully on Matipane Village in Limpopo Province. During the 2007 concert tour of the

John L. Spear

Kuyasa Kids (see detail in chapter five), Highland Park sponsored at least fifty children from Matipane and hosted a joint concert of Horizon's Kuyasa Kids with the Casper Children's Chorale at a local high school.

Northeast Community Church, Fishers, Indiana, Fred Bays, pastor. Persons from this congregation traveled with Horizon to South Africa and Zambia in November, 2008. They chose to partner with Derrick and Mercy Banda and Horizon's ministry through the Pentecostal Holiness Church in Chongwe District. Once home, travelers on this trip provided personal reports to the congregation over two Sundays, resulting in forty-six children being sponsored in Chongwe and the underwriting of regular support of the salaries of the Bandas. The missions chair, Travis Callaway, is now leading the effort and personally sponsors several children. A financial person professionally, he secured a grant to assist the travel of congregational members to Zambia to explore additional partnership possibilities. In 2010 he was named a new member of the Horizon board of directors.

Milo D. Miller

Travis Callaway

Northview Christian Life Church, Carmel, Indiana. Several partnerships have evolved in Sekgopo Village in South Africa's Limpopo Province, partly because the needs have been great and partly because it has been a relatively safe place to go and serve. The primary partnership in this village now is the Northview Christian Life Church in Carmel, Indiana, where Doug Ehrgott was the missions and outreach pastor before joining Horizon's leadership team in 2009.

Ehrgott went on a mission trip with Horizon and it changed his life and ministry focus. Soon Robert Pearson was invited to speak at Northview and the Kuyasa Kids came from South Africa and sang. On

Northview Christian Life Church, Carmel, Indiana

that one concert day with the Kuyasa Kids, one-hundred and five children in Sekgopo Village were sponsored! Other trips followed, one including a senior high group and worship band from the church to lead an Adventure Camp. Some songs were written from this experience and later included in a CD titled "With One Voice," now being sold to further assist Horizon's ministry.

Another element of this partner congregation is of special significance. This congregation placed Horizon in its capital funds campaign and promised $150,000 when success was reached, some of this to help finish construction of the Sekgopo Drop-In Center and perimeter fencing of that big property. Success has been achieved! This wonderful congregation took a Christmas offering in 2009 for Horizon's Children's Reserve Fund. It totaled $33,700.

Michael and Michelle Canada

Pendleton Christian Church, Pendleton, Indiana, Mike and Michelle Canada, pastors. This congregation has chosen to focus its Horizon-related mission service on Epworth Park in Harare,

190

Zimbabwe. When the Kuyasa Kids children's choir sang for the congregation in 2008, sixty-two children of Epworth Park were sponsored. In April, 2009, Horizon's Doug Ehrgott led a mission trip to Epworth Park, accompanied by the pastor's wife, Michelle Canada, and others from this congregation. Despite the carnage in this section of Harare in 2008, the ministry held together and this church's bond with it survived. In late 2009 the Canadas moved to leadership of a congregation in Lincoln, Nebraska, hoping to continue partnering from there with Horizon, likely in relation to Epworth Park in Harare, Zimbabwe. Meanwhile, the Pendelton congregation gave $29,000 for property to be used by a future school in Epworth Park.

Lloyd O. Bowen

Pleasant Prairie Church of God, Satanta, Kansas, Lloyd O. Bowen, pastor. Detail about this congregation's significant giving through Horizon to a range of urgent needs in Zimbabwe is found in chapter four. Bowen has been an enthusiastic participant in Horizon ministries.

These and dozens of other congregations from various Christian faith traditions across North America have joined Horizon International in its ministries in southern and eastern Africa. An image from the web site of the Church of God of Exeter, California, makes clear what Horizon and its many partnerships are all about. The twin purposes are to bring forth (1) a new generation of children saved from poverty, disease, and despair, and (2) a new generation so spiritually nurtured and educated that it is able to make a difference in the futures of struggling African nations. Purposes this large require that servants of Christ pour out themselves in loving ministry, trusting God for tomorrow.

Chapter Eight

BY ALL AVAILABLE MEANS

The care of orphans in desperate situations has always been at the heart of the mission of Horizon International. The singularity of this mission, however, does not limit the multiplicity of means employed to fulfill that mission. It does "take a village" to care for a child. So, on the one hand, the foundation has remained the sponsorship of children – covering basic health, housing, food, clothing, spiritual, and educational needs. But, in addition, the ministries of Horizon have come to include internships, adventure camps, pastor's conferences, microfinance loans and projects, sewing and welding schools, computer labs, calendars, catalogs, shipping containers, library books, and more.

These wide-ranging efforts of Horizon International are all complementary ways of offering a world of new hope to the youngest victims of the AIDS pandemic. Effective ministry for Horizon must be creative and flexible, but without ever losing sight of the orphans themselves!

Horizon International had begun its African ministry in Kayamandi township located in the Western Cape Province of South Africa. Its purpose was serving the immediate needs of AIDS orphans so common there. The means of serving that purpose would be styled to that particular set of circumstances.

In Kayamandi, the ministry style would be a home-based model, with a community center to support the many needs of the orphan

Ministries of Horizon International

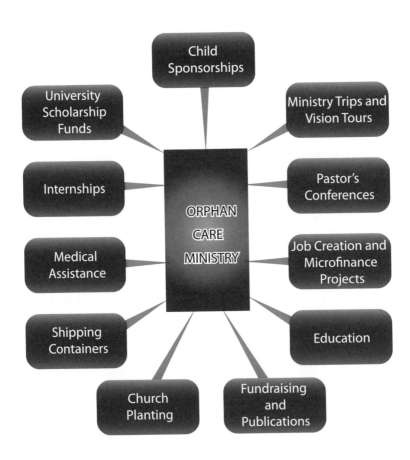

caregivers. Soon, however, the complexity of doing the job well became more and more apparent, as did the numerous ways needed to address the giant task with any sense of adequacy in multiple sets of circumstances. Particularly as Horizon's ministry spread beyond the nation of South Africa, the challenges grew ever greater, and the diverse ways of facing them also increased.

Faith and creativity were needed in large supply. Previous chapters have reviewed the reasons for launching new ministries and the key leaders and partners who have emerged to make it all possible, now in four different African countries and soon to be in five. Now comes less of the why, where, and who, and more of the *how*. How has Horizon and its African partners managed its effective work during this first decade of this ministry's life and service?

This chapter highlights some of what has developed along the way, *multiple* means of Christian ministry focused on a *single* goal. The center of Horizon's mission has remained the ministry of caring for children orphaned because of the HIV/AIDS pandemic; however, the means of such caring have become multiple in number and diverse in nature. The children are impacted by the whole social/political environment surrounding their fragile existence; therefore, adequate ministry to them requires various dimensions of "community transformation." Even more, the needs of the children range widely with the health, location, age, interests, and academic aptitude of each child.

Note the graphic on the opposite page. While a wide range of supportive ministries has evolved in Horizon's servant life, the care of orphans remains the central purpose, being implemented in various ways by each of the other ministries. What follows the graphic seeks to explain these several means of ministry.

INTERNS

The possibility soon arose for young Americans to begin serving through Horizon International as interns in Africa. The nature of Horizon's ministry and the severity of the human need being addressed combined to nurture missionary interest in the United States and to inspire gifted young people. The challenge facing Horizon, however, was investing the required time and finding the necessary wisdom to prepare such persons, however well motivated, to face numerous multi-cultural issues. In addition, ways had to be found to assist African-based staff persons in handling well the needs of young interns who might serve for short periods of time under their supervision. In its initial years of ministry, Horizon has had some outstanding successes with interns, and a few difficult learning experiences.

In the fall of 2003, Robert W. Pearson, Horizon's president, was visiting the Antelope Road Christian Fellowship in Citrus Heights, California. This was the congregation where, on his first visit in May, 2002, dozens of its members were impressed with the new ministry vision of Horizon and pledged to support monthly the first eighteen children to be sponsored by Horizon. Now Pearson was back, this time with Cassie and Jenny Carstens of South Africa. One of the congregation's college students, Cindy Nixon, was studying child development and asked if the new ministry could use an intern for a year at its Kayamandi ministry site in South Africa. This would be a first. All agreed on the idea, beginning a long relationship between Cindy and Horizon, and a pattern of future interns.

The actual launching of a program of Horizon interns came in the summer of 2004, with two goals in mind. The program would strengthen the service potential of available staff in South Africa and help develop potential young ministry leaders from the United States. The first intern to actually be deployed was Tammi Evans, a young woman from the Church of God (Anderson) congregation in Big Sandy, Montana. She had been a missions major in college and now spent ten weeks in Kayamandi township in South Africa, living with the Carstens, distributing 30,000 cartons of orange juice given to the ministry, and organizing an after-school Bible Club for local orphans. The orange juice got her into the high school, churches, and nearly everywhere else in Kayamandi – a very quick and good introduction to local ministry.

Then, in the fall of 2004, the second intern, Cindy Nixon, came from the Antelope Road Christian Fellowship in California. She had sensed while in high school a divine call to AIDS orphan ministry. While in college, Robert Pearson and the Carstens had made that visit to her congregation on behalf of Horizon. In a Sunday school class taught by Christopher Dancy, later a member of the board of directors of Horizon, the mission challenge was presented and Cindy inquired about the possibility of her becoming an intern in South Africa. The door was opened and she had begun fundraising to make this possible.

Cindy traveled to Kayamandi with a Horizon Vision Tour group and then remained for the year 2005, assisting the social worker with home visits. She helped new orphans with their grief process, and pioneered in a range of programmatic ways, including assisting with the Kuyasa Kids Choir as it was first forming and touring. She enrolled for training through Horizon's partner, the Africa Leadership Institute for Community Transformation (ALICT), preparing herself for a much longer stay in Africa than first expected. Since late 2007, Nixon has been a "staff missionary" of Horizon in Capetown, South Africa, Horizon's first such person. She now is married to a South African, Neal DeBeer, and is in charge of the Learning Center in Kayamandi township.

Cindy (Nixon) DeBeer, 2004

Looking ahead to 2006, the Horizon board of directors approved five young American women to serve in various internship roles in South Africa. Nixon had already completed a very successful year-long internship in Kayamandi, leading the Carstens to request her return. Each intern was responsible for securing funding and was required to sign an agreement form for mutual understanding and legal protection. Such persons offered fresh energy and idealism, and potentially would become enthusiastic spokespersons for Horizon following their service. The challenges, however, were great. Each intern required close staff supervision since she or he was young and facing significant cross-cultural demands personally. Most adjusted very well, although a few did not.

Twenty Horizon interns were deployed in 2007. One type of ministry internship was a short-term assignment for university students on summer vacation. The other involved a longer appointment for a year, maybe even longer if renewal was desired and warranted. One lesson learned from the early experiences with interns was that the cultural adjustment required is very demanding, and local supervisors are not always fully prepared to handle this process effectively.

For instance, two young women came home early from internships in Uganda. Two interns in Limpopo Province, South Africa, also had adjustment challenges, but managed them well enough to serve for about six months of the intended year. Horizon learned through these experiences that an internship training manual was needed and that interns should be deployed only in Horizon's more advanced ministry centers where quality supervision was readily available.

See the following graphic for a full listing of Horizon interns to date. Some of these, like Trysha Dancy and Dan Pentecost, had favorable experiences, ones that might even lead to decisions for mission careers in Africa later in life. Note the large change in the number of interns from 2007 to 2008. The new role of Doug and Sandy Ehrgott, full-time Global Team Builders with Horizon beginning in January, 2009, was intended in part to refine and strengthen the internship program.

Trysha Dancy

Dan Pentecost

198

INTERNS SERVING WITH HORIZON INTERNATIONAL

Years and Places of African Service

INTERNS	2004	2005	2006	2007	2008	2009
Centento, Erica				1		
Dancy, Trysha			1	1		
Demmer, Tara			1			
Evans, Tammi	1					
Geyer, Crystal			4			
Grable, Deanon				2		
Gretsch, Amber				1		
Hake, Jessie				2		
Harlow, Jennifer				1		
Harris, Brenton				1		
Hernandez, Ryan				1		
Jarros, Amanda				1		
Moser, Hannah				3		
Murnane, Katie					2	
Nelson, Stephanie						
Nixon, Cindy (DeBeer)	1	1	1	1		
Oliver, Heidi				3		
Parry, Elizabeth					1	
Pentecost, Dan					2	2
Peterson, Laura			1			
Richardson, Kimberly				1		

1. Western Cape Province, South Africa
2. Limpopo Province, South Africa
3. Southwestern Uganda
4. Natal Province, South Africa

ADVENTURE CAMPS

Horizon International's president, Robert Pearson, had been reared in the Church of God (Anderson), a revivalistic movement that often used church conventions, campmeetings, and youth summer camps to teach and evangelize. It was natural, then, for him to introduce a similar strategy in Africa where the orphaned children struggle daily with life in destructive environments, and rarely if ever have opportunity to leave them for personal refreshment.

The Horizon team soon judged that the sponsored children needed a time away from everything familiar. In a new setting, where full attention and fresh excitement was possible, Pearson hoped "to establish the spark that gets a raging fire going in somebody's life relative to Christ." Jenny Carstens had the original idea of this happening through short-term camps, with the first one to involve children from Kayamandi township.

In 2003, through special funding from Horizon donors, thirty orphans between the ages of ten and sixteen, participated in the first summer camp in the Western Cape conducted through *Kuyasa Horizon Empowerment*. Several of the Kayamandi kids committed their lives to Jesus Christ and began joyously singing songs like "Never Give Up!" (an early step toward the formation of the Kuyasa Kids Children's Choir – see chapter five). Then in August, 2005, at Horizon's African Staff Retreat that convened in Capetown, South Africa, there was extensive discussion about how to accomplish more than just care for the survival needs of sponsored orphans – particularly how to address their need for Jesus Christ and spiritual growth. The result was a determination to repeat the 2003 summer camp idea in various African locations.

These events, called "Adventure Camps," would be designed with three objectives in mind: (1) Teach the children about God as wonderfully known in Jesus Christ (their Bible knowledge was very limited); (2) Have frank discussions about sexuality (critical for responsible morality and avoiding the HIV infection); and (3) Encourage the children to participate in the afternoon children's clubs that meet throughout the year (providing both Bible teaching and English classes). Such camps were to become a regular occurrence in the

African life of Horizon. They were enthusiastically endorsed by Horizon's regional coordinators.

One way of funding these camps was through raising money from children in the United States. Horizon began encouraging congregations to expose American children to the plight of their African counterparts through their regular Vacation Bible School programming. Then the children could be challenged to give on behalf of these children. Kids love to give to other kids with whom they identify strongly. The particular goal was funding Adventure Camp scholarships for more and more needy African children. Such giving was encouraged by a growing number of stories of young Africans giving their lives to Jesus Christ in these settings and afterwards leading many of their friends to similar faith commitments.

Pendleton Christian Church members inspiring
children of Zimbabwe, 2009

Beyond crucial faith commitments, another need is critical and is being faced openly with the children during these camp experiences. Sexual purity of the young is crucial in the overall fight to contain the spread of AIDS and to promote a responsible Christian lifestyle. As early as June, 2005, *Kuyasa Horizon Empowerment's* Cindy Nixon and Mbongeni Mtshali had taken a group of children from Kayamandi township in South Africa to a youth event featuring *The Silver Ring Thing*. This was a Christian group traveling internationally to promote sexual abstinence before marriage, sex God's way.

Unfortunately, premarital and casual sex is ingrained in the Kayamandi township youth culture, often with devastating results. At the end of *The Silver Ring Thing* program, a call was issued for kids to stand in front of their peers and make a purity commitment. All seventeen of the Horizon kids stood to their feet! They purchased purity rings and knew that they would be helped to learn more about Jesus and his will for their lives. Adequate ministry to AIDS orphans must include such a dimension.

A set of Adventure Camps was reported in the February, 2007, Horizon newsletter sent across North America. In Limpopo Province, South Africa, Horizon's regional coordinators Andries and Nelly van der Merwe had overseen two groups of sponsored orphan children, about sixty in all, going to camp by appropriate age groups. They had been taken to Wisa Kurula, a game lodge catering to church groups, in different weeks in December, 2006. Beyond just plain fun, the camp program had focused on AIDS awareness, sexual abstinence, life skills, and Bible study. Most of the children had made "purity commitments" (abstinence before marriage) and received purity commitment certificates. Each had received a personal Bible provided by Highland Park Community Church in Casper, Wyoming. When each of the camps had concluded, none of the children wanted to go home!

Another Adventure Camp was convened in 2007 in western Uganda, with four hundred young Africans attending – some orphans being sponsored through Horizon and others waiting for that privilege. Aides to the office of Uganda's president were present, thus becoming acquainted with Horizon in their country and encouraging various ways

Children listen, learn, and grow in Adventure Camps

that the national government might become involved in this ministry. Still another camp, this one in Limpopo Province, South Africa, involved about twenty-five African youth and nearly the same number of youth from the Northview Christian Life Church in Carmel, Indiana. This American congregation paid for the scholarships necessary for the participating South African children. Emerging from this life-changing

Gayla Morgan, Horizon's Child Sponsorship Coordinator

experience at the Magnab Safari Lodge was a recording titled *With One Voice*. It was put together by Josh Cecil and his worship band from the Carmel congregation. Included was a song by Kayla Schaaf celebrating a relationship developed in this wonderful camp experience.

MICROFINANCE

In March, 2005, the Horizon board of directors discussed at length the potential strategy of microfinancing for supporting the mission of Horizon. Other ministries had proven that offering small loans to worthy persons in a developing country can generate new businesses, stimulate community transformation, and benefit directly an organization's primary ministry.

Could microfinance work effectively in support of Horizon's orphan care? To answer this question, the board approved in concept the addition of microfinancing to Horizon's range of ministries, noting that the board would insist on approving in advance the business plan for every major microfinance project proposed in the future.

A Horizon-related economic development program was soon launched in southwest Uganda. It quickly became one of the more promising of the many Horizon ministries there. This microfinance initiative had been encouraged by Michael Carey, a project manager and donor to Horizon who had significant background in such matters. The Careys had come to Horizon in 2005 as retired public school teachers in Casper, Wyoming. They had become committed Christians later in life through the pastoral ministries of John Spear and Milo Miller at the Highland Park Church of God in Casper.

Mike Carey became a stockbroker and worked

at developing various fundraising skills that could assist Christian not-for-profit ministries. He traveled to Africa, saw Horizon's ministries and their leaders firsthand, and was very impressed with the unusual intelligence and commitment of these leaders. He then offered this judgment: "It was obvious that God was in Horizon. It's rapid growth is just not normal for new not-for-profits." While helping in the early computerizing of Horizon's home offices in Pendleton, Indiana, his heart was now in Africa. He and Diane began being generous with Horizon in many ways. She began a prayer ministry in direct support of Horizon. His particular interest was in making the African ministries economically sustainable. Microfinance was a strategy he knew well and encouraged.

Horizon now has a microfinance program. It is a ministry of empowerment, a cost-effective way to help some of Africa's poorest people start or build up small businesses that can support them, their loved ones, and orphans they dedicate themselves to serve. Beginning in southwest Uganda, this program was designed to provide low-interest loans to enable the launching of small new businesses. It soon was registered with the Ugandan government to do business as the *Covenant Savings and Credit Society*. It functions as a subsidiary of *Horizon Uganda*.

The major target group for the Society's loans are care-givers to Horizon-sponsored orphans, and also older orphans who have graduated from their Horizon sponsorships and need ways to proceed with a stable and productive adulthood. The goal is moving recipients from dependence to interdependence, and eventually to self-reliance. Mike Carey of Horizon echoed the general philosophy of Horizon's microfinance ministry – "It's a great thing to help people learn to help themselves!"

The Ugandan microfinance ministry began in 2006 with Horizon providing loans of $100 each to thirteen orphan caregivers. By September, 2008, the Covenant Savings and Credit Society had two full-time employees and was serving thirty-eight community-based groups in six districts of southwestern Uganda. It had a total membership of 1,450 individual and family units, with Horizon's direct financial contributions exceeding $5,000. Loans are granted to qualified persons and usually are to be paid back in a year or less at two percent interest.

The total loan portfolio of the Society has grown to 20 million Ugandan shillings per year (about $12,500). One early beneficiary was Irene Katuutu Mobiiho, a Horizon care-giver. She used her loan to purchase a bale of used clothing and then set up a booth in Fort Portal's public market. A year later she was able to move to a storefront in the commercial district, opening *Irene's Boutique.* Other loan

recipients have opened produce stalls, launched craft-making businesses and animal husbandry projects, etc.

One congregation in North America really caught the microfinance ministry vision. The First Church of God in Alma, Michigan, and its pastor Steve Wimmer, decided to channel through Horizon its Christmas donations of about $3,800 in 2007 and $4,100 in 2008. They were soon used to help Songo start a goat herd, Ednasi to plant a corn field, Angeli to sell fish and vegetables at a roadside stand, and Rehema to launch a used clothing business. Rev. Wimmer had demonstrated to his congregation in an unusual way the significance of this microfinance program.

Steve D. Wimmer

Thirteen people of the Alma, Michigan, congregation were asked to come to the platform. Their pastor explained that Horizon had earlier provided $100 loans to each of them. One Ugandan had used the money to start a chicken business and another a necklace business. Since ten of the thirteen had now repaid their loans from early profits, the pastor asked three of the people to return to their seats. Ten new persons joined the ten who had repaid, symbolizing a recycling of the original loans. This was repeated, now with thirty adults standing before the church, all funded by the initial $1,300.

Even the children of this congregation grasped the idea when illustrated so vividly. Gifts could be multiplied again and again, resulting in an amazing array of businesses that could sustain adults and care for desperate children. The Alma congregation had set in motion what might be generations of revolving loans, and also had purchased a motorcycle for the loan officer servicing the ministry. The people were thrilled by the substantial impact of their generosity, and then proceeded to give an additional $4,000 to Horizon's microfinance ministry so that more orphan caregivers could help themselves and others by starting new businesses.

Pastor's Conferences

When Horizon began sponsoring orphans in the Mt. Darwin area of Zimbabwe, it was obvious that there were too few congregations and pastors in that area to support the larger effort necessarily involved in caring for the area's orphans. Planting churches thus became a Horizon priority, as did the training of pastors to lead them. After all, how could sponsored orphans be nurtured spiritually without pastors, or with poorly prepared pastors? Horizon's mission was more than filling empty stomachs and giving clothes, medicine, and safe shelter to orphans. It also was to raise up a new generation of young Christians for the future of Africa.

A goal of this magnitude will not be accomplished easily. It will take the presence of many well-prepared Christian pastors. Horizon team members and American visitors observed evidence of real need among such Christian leaders. For instance, they saw four pastors in the Mt. Darwin area sharing one Bible – they had torn it into sections and were trading them back and forth! This was judged intolerable! Soon one hundred new Bibles were purchased and delivered by Horizon team members.

Then in November, 2006, Horizon sponsored a pastor's conference to teach basic Christian theology to fifty-three Shona pastoral couples in Harare, Zimbabwe. Another conference was staged for dozens of Xhosa pastoral couples in Kayamandi township in the Western Cape Province of South Africa. A third pastor's conference, this time in Uganda, was planned and promised to have a very large number of pastors participating. In fact, the number turned out to be 2,200 coming from the western Uganda area! This three-day conference, convened in November, 2007, was the largest single event in Horizon's history to that time. Groups who were represented among the participants ranged from Anglican priests to Pentecostals and even Muslims desiring more information about Jesus.

A highlight of the conference was when Robert Pearson was speaking. He felt inspired to call appreciative attention to the elderly care-givers of Horizon who were present, those who were serving the orphans on a daily basis and rarely were celebrated in any circle. Most

Robert Pearson honoring elderly Horizon caregivers

were grandparents whose children were dead and who now were raising the grandchildren with Horizon's assistance. It was a moving scene.

Pearson reports what happened this way: "About seventy elderly men and women walked forward at my invitation, and I was blown away. It was one of those holy God moments, an awesome time I will remember for the rest of my life. The crowd rose to applaud them, and then I prayed that God would provide for their needs as they so faithfully were providing for others."

The theme for this very large Ugandan pastor's conference was "The God Who Speaks, Summons, Serves, and Sends." The curriculum had been developed by Todd Faulkner as part of his doctoral work at Anderson University's School of Theology. His doctoral dissertation is titled "Narrative Theology for the Practice of Ministry." It includes units that employ visually-oriented biblical and theological concepts. This story-telling style of teaching/learning fit the African context very well. Faulkner is now the campus pastor of Anderson University and continues to seek ways to assist Horizon's ministry. Michael Henderson, the executive director of Horizon's partner, *Heart of Africa*, helped raise funding for this major teaching event, while Horizon's regional coordinators in Uganda, Silas and Betty Atugonza, carried responsibility for the considerable logistics.

An urgent circumstance then forced its way forward in early 2009, crying out for Horizon's assistance. Scores of Horizon-related pastors in Zimbabwe had been intimidated, the lives of their congregations disrupted, and some even beaten brutally as part of the political turmoil in that country. A Horizon team risked travel and hardship to convene a pastor's conference in February to bring encouragement and guidance to courageous Christian leaders (more on this historic conference is found in chapter four). God obviously was in this effort. The tide of evil was turning, finally, toward a time of new hope and ministry. A key part of the turn was the presence of newly encouraged and equipped Christian pastors.

The concept behind these pastor's conferences has been the recruiting of American pastors and congregational leaders to do the teaching, with the goal of preparing better-trained African leaders, particularly the ones who direct congregations where Horizon's sponsored children worship and are spiritually nurtured. A helpful byproduct, of course, has been that the teachers, having been exposed to

Horizon's African ministries, have tended to go home and enlist their congregations as active Horizon supporters.

The urgent need in Zimbabwe (see chapter six) offered the opportunity for crisis intervention. Help came from an unexpected source, a small rural congregation in Kansas, U.S.A. Here is a good example of the participation of one committed church leader leading to more inspired ministry on the part of others back home. An Horizon pastor's conference was convened in Harare, Zimbabwe, in February, 2009. Part of the teaching team was Lloyd Bowen, pastor of the Pleasant Prairie Church of God in Satanta, Kansas. He had been encouraged to become involved by Horizon's president, Robert Pearson. This congregation generously supported its pastor's trip and his roles of teaching and leading devotionals during this conference. The timing was critical for the well being of the churches in Zimbabwe. The pastors attending had been threatened and many physically beaten by government-inspired militias during the recent political upheaval, so it was time for healing, teaching, and inspiring.

Bowen guided worship sessions around the theme "Lessons Out of the Psalms of Pain" and taught from Nehemiah 4 on "What To Do When Opposition Arises." His heart broke as he saw that many of these pastors had no Bible of their own, or only part of one from which to study and minister. Once home, he told this sad story and soon raised an additional $4,000 to allow the printing and delivery to these pastors in Zimbabwe of many new Thompson Chain Reference Bibles. Even more money was raised in this Kansas congregation to provide scholarships for the pastors. In just the first months of 2009, this one rural church gave some $10,000 to Horizon ministries in Zimbabwe – and with wonderful results!

A Maze of "Cs"

Horizon International seeks to aid its many African orphans by all available means. "C" words have come to represent the wide range of practical approaches beyond standard sponsorships of individual children. There now are catalogs, containers, calendars, contests, CDs, and more.

The 2008 calendar of Horizon International went on sale in 2007, with all proceeds going to support future Adventure Camps for African orphans. It and the one for 2009 were rich in photography of young

Africans being saved from desperation and preparing to be the next generation of leaders. They were being taught to love their home countries, gain skills that can bring viable living and thus new hope, and fill their hearts with Jesus Christ, who is at the center of all hope for the children and their countries.

In early November, 2007, some 12,000 copies of Horizon's 2008 Christmas catalog were sent to churches and individuals. An order form and return envelope were enclosed, as were instructions for buying online. Here, it was said, was "a way to make a world of difference a world away." The dozens of available options ranged widely. Ten dollars could buy a Bible in English or a tribal language – every Horizon child is to get one! A dozen mosquito nets for $144 could protect that many children from malaria, a leading cause of death among the young children in Africa. As little as $75 would buy a share in the purchase of computers and software for new labs in Fort Portal, Uganda, and Harare,

Zimbabwe.
One chicken for hungry Zimbabwe could be purchased for $15, providing eggs so that children could have healthy breakfasts and meat for lunches and suppers.

There was more, much more in that catalog. There were bicycles, university scholarships, sewing machines, even hippo water rollers for $100 each. These are simple devices that allow even an aging caregiver to roll many gallons of water from the nearest source to a humble residence. Another $100 could buy a share in a new veggie tunnel, a small greenhouse that can be placed conveniently on a small plot of land to grow vegetables quickly. The challenge of this 2008 Christmas catalog was for North Americans to purchase items in the names of people on their Christmas shopping lists. Instead of buying things not necessarily desired or needed, people could choose to honor their loved ones and, in the process, make a world of difference a world away.

Young people were emerging with energy, creativity, and commitment to Horizon's cause. The 2002 bike-a-thon on behalf of Horizon was ridden from Lexington, Kentucky, to Bangor, Maine, and then featured in *Adventure Cycling* magazine. The "Teetering for Tots" one-hundred-hour marathon was staged by a student group at Anderson University and raised $5,400. The Los Angeles "Run to the Horizon" marathon included the participation of twenty-nine students of Azusa Pacific University and was inspired by student Alex Shute who was from the First Church of God in Houston, Texas.

Alex Shute

Shute had first heard Horizon's Robert Pearson preach in his Texas

Logo of Horizon in the Los Angeles Marathon

home church when he was about fourteen. Then in 2005 Horizon's Kuyasa Kids Choir was touring the United States and sang in his church. Two of the African boys stayed in the Shute home. That is when Alex began thinking about how he could get involved with Horizon's ministry. What was Shute's motivation? He said, "I primarily want people, Christians in particular, to be aware that we are One Body, as referred to in Ephesians. When one part of the body hurts, the entire body hurts. I want students in Africa to be able to pursue their dreams and affect their home communities for Christ." Alex was echoing the voice of Horizon itself. In fact, he went on to graduate from Azusa Pacific University and spend several months as a World Vision intern in Rwanda, working with microfinance projects – and he has interest in assisting with Horizon's microfinance program in Uganda.

The month of April, 2008, was the time of opportunity for Grace Sharritt and other students at Pendleton Heights High School in Indiana to get involved in frontier ministry. Located adjacent to the home offices of Horizon in Pendleton, this high school was the scene of students organizing and successfully pulling off a twenty-four-hour walk-a-thon around the school track. They repeated the event the next year, raising a

Grace Sharritt

total of more than $13,000 for Horizon's kids, particularly for Horizon's University Scholarship Endowment Fund (see chapter nine). Then came a special treat. The Kuyasa Kids from South Africa came on tour in that area and sang for the organizing high school group. Sharritt reports that she was thrilled and grateful to God "for this amazing opportunity to do a good thing, to be part of something larger than myself."

Such events would be repeated, and with other kinds of fundraising efforts also emerging. For example, a contest was staged among three Sunday school classes from three different congregations. The goal was to raise funds for two of Horizon's field teams to purchase new laptop computers so that they could use them for their ministries. The proud winner was Culver City Church of God in Los Angeles, California, that raised $2,000. The Sunday school teacher, Walter Broadwell, said that "showing love in this way not only rescues the children, but provides a strong witness to what the love of Jesus Christ means."

In the summer of 2008 the city school system in Anderson, Indiana, was recycling all of its English textbooks (literature and grammar). Jan Callen, a member of the English faculty at Anderson High School and wife of Horizon board member Barry L. Callen, was part of the November, 2007, Vision Tour of Horizon that brought her into contact and instant friendship with Nyembezi Siziba. This young Zimbabwean woman teaches English at the Nyamahobogo Secondary School in the rural Mt. Darwin area. Siziba had motivated students with proper uniforms, but with limited food and clean water at the school, and with no English textbooks. While Horizon determined to address the water issue, Jan Callen was burdened about the textbook and school library issue.

Late 2008 and the early part of 2009 saw teachers across Zimbabwe not functioning in the schools. They had not been paid and just could not go on that way. Then a fragile power-sharing political arrangement was made in Harare between President Magabe and his determined opposition leaders. Attention finally was given to getting the schools reopened. When the Nyamahobogo school opened again, Nyembezi Siziba, recently married, had a large supply of English textbooks to use, compliments of Horizon International and the loving initiative of Jan Callen and others. The school property was being gifted to Horizon's partner organization, *Voice of Peace,* by local officials. This would release Horizon to go to the considerable expense of drilling a new well so that clean water could be available to the students and faculty. Quality education now has a chance at a genuinely new beginning.

Jan Callen and Nyembezi Siziba

How did all these English textbooks, 125,000 freeze-dried meals, and quantities of various other things get delivered from the United States to Zimbabwe? The inspiration came from Tracy Christian who found a funding source and arranged for a shipping container that could carry everything. It was filled, crossed the eastern United States by train, and then crossed the Atlantic Ocean by ship, before being put back on a train in Africa on its way finally to Harare, Zimbabwe. It took many strong hands, big Christian hearts, a generous businessman in Michigan, and thousands of miles, but it got done for the good of children and the glory of God. Tracy Christian, in addition to this container, has served Horizon as a volunteer recruiter of child sponsors in Kansas City and has sponsored several fundraising events.

The mission goal of Horizon is to serve the needs of orphans. The means to meet this goal have turned out to be several, each seeking to match one of the complex elements of the need with a place-specific and timely approach. Regardless of whatever has emerged as necessary, Horizon has sought to be flexible, creative, and faithful to the goal. Partners in North America and Africa have shared their gifts, ideas, time, and hearts. God has blessed them and the ministry.

Doug Ehrgott

Chapter Nine

LAUNCHING INTO TOMORROW

While Horizon International is already an amazing story of God's work in the midst of a human tragedy of almost unimaginable proportions, the story has only begun. This tenth-anniversary volume traces the beginnings and first years of major expansion, but so much obviously lies ahead. Reaching the milestone of a first decade has provided an excellent time to stop, remember, and rejoice. It also is a good time to look forward.

This final chapter notes early efforts to tell the Horizon story, and it explains select strategies now in process for enhancing future ministry on behalf of the orphans now graduating from Horizon's care. It also looks at how Horizon's leaders intend to stay open to God as the divinely intended future keeps unfolding.

President Robert Pearson recalls something once said in his hearing by a favorite Bible professor: "If you want to get close to God, find out what is near to his heart, and then go and camp out there." Fortunately, the Bible makes very clear something that lies close to the divine heart. Said Jesus: "Let the little children come to me, and do not hinder them, for the kingdom of God belongs to such as these" (Matt. 10:14). The place of the outcast, the ill, the forgotten, especially when they are children, is where we should camp out. God will be there! By God's grace, Horizon International will be there too.

Another wise statement comes from Phillips Brooks, the great New England preacher: "You never become truly spiritual by sitting down and wishing to become so. You must undertake something so great that you cannot accomplish it unaided." Therefore, another question faces us. Do we want to become spiritual, getting close to God? Then, as far as Horizon is concerned, we must go to the desperate children of Africa, camp lovingly with them, and attempt something beyond our human ability. We must address the devastating AIDS pandemic and raise up a new generation of young Africans who will embrace life in Jesus Christ and bring a new day to their struggling nations.

That is an assignment so great that Horizon International cannot possibly begin to accomplish it without considerable assistance. Accordingly, beginning in 2001, Horizon has set up camp near God's heart, found God with the children, and begun accomplishing the impossible task--with divine aid, of course, and with the assistance of many African partners. It is an ongoing journey of faith, one that has only just begun.

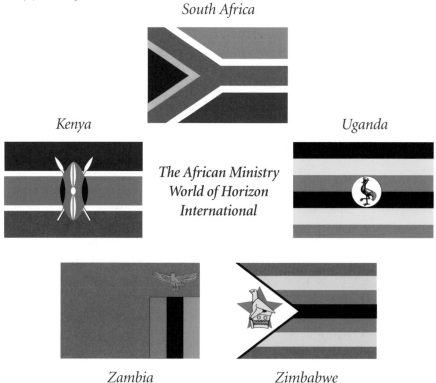

South Africa

Kenya

The African Ministry World of Horizon International

Uganda

Zambia

Zimbabwe

Telling Horizon's Story

A central challenge from almost day one of Horizon's existence has been achieving an effective system of communication with its ever-growing constituencies. Almost as important as what gets accomplished is who learns about the accomplishments and the urgent challenges now faced by the ministry, and how effectively they are told. The effectiveness of the communication often determines whether or not those many people "out there" become motivated to join the ministry through their dollars and other means of participation. The future depends in part on learning about the past. Ownership of the ministry relies on good communication.

It has been fortunate that Robert Pearson, Horizon's founder and president, is an effective public speaker and skillful writer. In the September 8, 2007, meeting of Horizon's board of directors, he distributed new print materials recently developed under his supervision to support the child sponsorship program. He also showed promotional materials for the upcoming concert tour of the Kuyasa Kids from South Africa and gave updated information on the Pendleton staff of Horizon – all very positive communication developments, primarily the work of staff person Amanda Scott. The materials included a child sponsor introductory packet, a 2008 Horizon calendar mock-up, Kuyasa Kids Tour promotional material, a vision tour/work camp brochure, and the beginnings of a Christmas catalog – a first for Horizon.

The Christmas catalog was mailed to everyone on Horizon's general and child sponsor mailing lists – approximately 2,500 families – and was distributed to every family of the large Northview Christian Life Church in Carmel, Indiana. It featured numerous potential Christmas gifts to be given in someone's honor in North America, and then usually purchased and delivered to a needy person in Africa. The items available included everything from animals and farming supplies to desks and computer equipment and software. The 2008 Horizon calendar sold for $20, with proceeds going to Horizon's Adventure Camp Scholarship Fund. The Houston, Texas, company of Matt Vere graciously donated the printing service. The music DVD titled *With One Voice* featured original worship music from the group *North Beach* of the Northview Christian Life Church of Carmel, Indiana. All proceeds from sales became gifts to Horizon.

For ease and effectiveness of communication, e-newsletters became a regular feature of Horizon's work. In December, 2005, Horizon's board of directors authorized the employment of Sean Sheridan and *4-Minute Media*, Colorado Springs, Colorado, to produce a four-color promotional brochure and a quality DVD of Horizon's Adventure Camps, showing the children committing their lives to Jesus Christ and giving their testimonies. The idea was to ship the DVDs to hundreds of congregational mission committees and leaders of Vacation Bible Schools in the United States, introducing Horizon and inspiring American children of privilege to share with African children in great need. Sheridan also made a major contribution to Horizon's web site (*www.horizoninternationalinc.com*) and in 2009 was contracted to travel back to Africa to shoot video for a new DVD that features the wonderful story of Trinity, an orphan sponsored personally by Sheridan. A complimentary copy of this DVD is found in the back of this book. Don't miss seeing it!

The beginning of 2009 saw Horizon International deploying a series of field representatives to service supporting churches and cultivate new ones. President Robert Pearson had been fulfilling this vital role personally since Horizon's beginning. He had traveled the country preaching in pulpits, relating to pastors, and meeting with mission committees. When the Kuyasa Kids Choir from South Africa began touring the United States, it naturally played a vital communication role. New churches were anxious to have them come. Once they did come and sing, the churches were inspired to join Horizon's ministry. For some years, Daniel Murrell and Jerry Jones had provided field assistance, primarily in the Indiana area. By 2009, however, the size and complexity of Horizon's organization and ministries required major assistance with field representation and other communication tasks.

Horizon's American staff in 2009 had come to include a network of field representatives, women and men who were introduced to the board of directors by president Pearson in September, 2008. They were called "a vey exciting lineup of individuals and couples who feel called to join our North American Horizon team and are committed to raising part of their own support." The group included Winston and Nancy Clark, field representatives for southern Indiana and Ohio.

The Clarks had concluded many years of pastoral ministry and now had been gripped by the divine vision and mission strategy of Horizon. They knew that God is the "Father of the fatherless" (Ps. 68:5), and they were excited that they were being sent to pastors and congregations to build a larger and deeper infrastructure for Horizon. As they raised the necessary support for their own financial needs, they were made aware by God that they were really raising hope for African orphans. Thus, field representatives, so far as they were concerned, could better be called "ambassadors of hope."

The Horizon staff group included Timothy and Cynthia Kumfer, field representatives for northern Indiana and Michigan, and Jay and Teresa Davidson, field representatives for Iowa and Wisconsin. Also included were Doug and Sandy Ehrgott who began full-time with Horizon in January, 2009, as Global Team Builders, bringing to Horizon and its president considerable administrative support by coordinating African trips and internships. They had served as the Missions and Outreach pastors at Northview Christian Life Church in Carmel, Indiana, a large congregation deeply involved in the ministries of Horizon.

Even more additions to the Horizon staff are coming. On the African front, serious consideration is being given to a new position, the "African Coordinator," someone who would serve as the liaison between Horizon International in the United States and the current and emerging ministry partners in the several African countries. On the American front, Horizon's board of directors, on September 20, 2008, formally commissioned the writing and publishing in 2010 of a major history book of Horizon International.

This present volume, *Hope on the Horizon*, is the result of that 2008 board action. It is a recounting and celebration of the amazing initial years of the ministry's existence and service, a path of self-giving clearly inspired by God and rendered on behalf of the desperate children of southern and eastern Africa. In its meeting on December 5, 2009, the board affirmed final details of this book's publishing and viewed the new DVD to be placed in the back of every copy. It presents vividly the story of Trinity, one of the many young Africans whose lives have been transformed because of the presence of Horizon International.

ENDOWMENT FOR HIGHER EDUCATION

Endowing a fund is a deliberate investment for the long-term future. An organization sets aside a portion of its own current finances or receives designated funds from others and dedicates their earnings (but not the principle) to one or more purposes vital to that donor and consistent with the organization's mission. In December, 2006, the Horizon board of directors established a general-fund endowment and directed that all monetary resources received in the future from wills or estates would be placed in this fund. Then in February, 2007, the board, with the general-fund endowment standing at a modest $3,000, directed that this and future fund assets should be invested in the "Founding Funds Strategy" of Franklin Templeton.

In addition to this general-fund endowment, Horizon had earlier established another endowment fund for a particular purpose, that of the continuing education of select graduates of Horizon's child sponsorship program. Some orphaned children who complete high school and then leave Horizon's formal sponsorship program are appropriate candidates for a university education – should such somehow be possible? The goal for this second endowment fund, therefore, was to address the urgent needs of those who are candidates for higher education.

Meranda Ramabale is one orphan who got sidetracked in life. She committed her life to Jesus Christ during a Horizon Adventure Camp in 2005. She lived with her grandmother and two sisters in Kgapane Village in Limpopo Province, South Africa. These three children had been sponsored through Horizon since the summer of 2003. They excelled in the local school system. Meranda, now a sincere Christian, dreamed of attending a South African university to become a dietician, thus being able to help at-risk children with nutritional meals. Unfortunately, she became pregnant during her final year in school. Her test scores were not good enough to qualify her for university scholarships, and with her baby she couldn't go anyway.

What could be salvaged from this negative circumstance? Many people who had been very excited about Meranda's future were disappointed. Though very shy and deeply saddened herself, Meranda successfully gave birth, became a devoted teenage mother, and began working with the area Horizon coordinators as a speaker about teenage pregnancies and related issues that are a curse to the local population. She soon reached thousands of people in schools, youth clubs, and by door-to-door contact, bringing them information and personal testimony on health, abstinence, and moral values. Meranda was finding ways to bring light out of the darkness of her own personal circumstances.

Other Horizon children of special academic promise have not gotten sidetracked by social ills so common in their culture. President Pearson was often asked by some of these older sponsored orphans if it would be possible for them to study at the university level. Part of Horizon's mission, after all, is to raise up a new generation of Christian leaders in Africa. But how could Horizon help finance select graduates of its own program for university educations? It would have to be through a University Scholarship Endowment Fund of Horizon.

The death of Arlene Callen, wife of board member Barry L. Callen, came in March, 2003. In her honor, Barry made a contribution to establish the Arlene Callen Memorial Fund, a perpetual endowment fund intended to generate earnings that would keep replacing sold inventories of Horizon's *Out of Africa Gift Shop*. This would help provide productive employment for disadvantaged Africans now related to Horizon's ministry. Arlene had a missionary heart; thus, this fund was intended as a fitting and perpetual memorial.

The memorial, however, would shift in focus in the years ahead. After an initial burst of excitement and local success, it became clear by early 2006 that the shop did not produce enough income to warrant the amount of expense and staff time required. So the board of directors decided to phase out this operation in its original form. The new form eventually would be an internet gift shop on Horizon's web site, with many of the goods also sold around the United States at concerts of the Kuyasa Kids Children's Choir and as part of local church presentations of Horizon's ministries. The endowment dollars originally invested in honor of Arlene Callen were moved, with Barry Callen's full blessing, to lay the early foundation of Horizon's University Scholarship Endowment Fund.

Future contributions to this University Fund would come from various sources. One was a major monetary gift of $20,000 from the estate of Barbara Hooper, a former educator in Colorado who knew the value of higher education and wanted the disadvantaged of Africa to have such an opportunity. But more than estate money was on its way to help fund the future education of orphaned African children who possess particular academic ability.

After Robert Pearson preached in a Horizon-supporting church in January, 2003, a high school student, Alex Shute, approached him expressing thanks for Horizon's ministry to AIDS orphans. Then in May, 2005, two members of the Kuyasa Kids Choir stayed in the Shute home. Alex told them that he was about to become a student at Azusa Pacific University in California. They were silent, dramatizing for him that they had no hope of going to any such school. Later, as an APU student with his own financial needs, Shute called the Horizon offices in Indiana to ask if he could run in the Los Angeles Marathon to raise money for the University Scholarship Endowment Fund. The answer, of course, was "Yes!" Before he was done with his project, he had recruited twenty-nine other APU students into a "Run to the Horizon" campaign. It raised thousands of dollars for the educational futures of African children. In April, 2008, Robert Pearson spoke to the student body of Azusa Pacific University and told Alex's story. Many came up to him and said they also would run for Horizon. More on the Shute story, and a similar one about Grace Sharritt, is found in chapter eight.

As of September, 2008, the University Scholarship Endowment Fund had grown to over $50,000, with efforts underway to increase this number considerably. That year the first scholarship was awarded, $1,200 for Rodney Sekhwela to study engineering and geology at the University of Pretoria in South Africa. His moving story represents so many others.

Rodney Sekhwela

Rodney was fourteen when he was first sponsored by Horizon in 2003. He was born and reared in Kgapane Village, Limpopo Province, South Africa. When he first met Horizon officials, president Robert Pearson and child sponsor coordinator Joyce

Chapple, he was living alone in the modest little house of his recently-deceased grandmother. He had not eaten for three days. Joyce felt led of God to sponsor him personally. He later graduated with honors from Kgapane High School.

Rodney was delighted, even ecstatic upon receiving news of a university scholarship granted to him from Horizon. In 2009 Horizon awarded him a second scholarship to continue in school. He completed an internship in geological mining and then began his senior year with Horizon's encouragement. Even though, in order to save money, he had to live in a shack community filled with refugees from Zimbabwe, Rodney survived, full of prayer, gratitude, and potential. He graduated in December, 2009, the first of Horizon's sponsored children to complete a program of higher education. He became employed in the same outstanding company where he had done his internship.

Rodney is a high academic achiever, the first of many others soon to follow. One certainly would be Confidence Tobo from Kayamandi Township in the Western Cape Province of South Africa. Her Horizon sponsor is none other than Horizon's president, Robert Pearson. He funded the tuition required for her to transfer to a prestigious high school in South Africa, positioning her for a probable full scholarship to the University of Stellenbosch upon high school graduation. Another outstanding achiever is Jennifer Maake.

By 2002, the parents of Jennifer Maake were gone, two more victims of the HIV/AIDS pandemic. Then age twelve, she felt like she had lost everything. Her unusual intelligence seemed almost a curse since there appeared to be no opportunity to develop and use such ability. Then Horizon sponsors appeared for her and her sister. Love, care, food, clothing, and, especially important for Jennifer, schooling became available. She eventually graduated with the highest grade-point average in the history of Sekgopo Village in Limpopo, Province, South Africa, a village of over 30,000 people.

There had been a time when Jennifer had blamed God for the frustration of being intelligent in a set of circumstances designed to keep intelligence from flowering. After Horizon's intervention and high school graduation, her dream was an actual possibility. She longs to be a civil engineer and now has been accepted as a student by an internationally renowned engineering school in Johannesburg. Horizon will remain by her side as she continues this journey from severely limited circumstances to the fulfillment of her potential.

Jennifer Maake

An expanding program of general-fund and scholarship endowments, accounts with great potential for growth, requires creative initiatives to cultivate gifts, express gratitude to donors, distribute earned revenues appropriately, and maximize the earning potential of the invested funds. So, in 2008, the Horizon board of directors established a modest administrative fee to be drawn from future contributions so that much more could be raised and effectively employed. The board was determined that the Horizon endowment funds would keep growing and providing support for ongoing ministry operations and the education of future Christian leaders for southern and eastern Africa.

In its meeting of December 5, 2009, two additional actions by the board of directors promised increased substance for this growth goal. One was the establishment of "The Tenfold Team." Persons would be challenged to give $10 per month to the University Scholarship Endowment Fund, and even recruit ten of their friends to do the same. How could Horizon do any less when hundreds, no, thousands of gifted young persons like the four young men pictured from Uganda are waiting to be released to the future? President Pearson interviewed these four men in 2008, all part of Horizon's sponsorship ministry in western Uganda since 2005. Each of them has a heart-wrenching story of personal loss in the past. What so impressed Pearson, however, was that, despite everything, each of them has a dream for the future. One intends to be an engineer, one a teacher, and two medical doctors. Each is determined and, with Horizon's help, has a real chance of making it!

The second significant action taken by Horizon's board of directors on December 5, 2009, was related to something very personal that

Edmond Kasule, Ronald Kato, Jumah Kitalengwa, and Joseph Mutegeki

recently had occurred in the life of president Robert Pearson. He had married Christine Herr in September. She is a health care professional who, once learning of Horizon's ministry, became inspired to seek new funding. She hoped it would come from the medical community of central Indiana to build a Health Services Scholarship Endowment Fund for appropriate orphans graduating from Horizon's child sponsorship program. The board of directors acted to launch such a fund, expressing deep appreciation for the vision and caring heart of Christine (Herr) Pearson. Resources generated will be used exclusively to enable select Horizon orphans in Africa to pursue medical training of various kinds.

Some graduates from Horizon's child sponsorship program will go on to study at some of Africa's finest universities. The fact is, however, that many of the orphans do not have the inclination or aptitude for studying successfully at the university level – but they would make great auto mechanics, seamstresses, carpenters, or welders, if given the chance to train in a vocational setting that could be afforded. Two examples highlight Horizon's initiative in this area (and there are others in various stages of development).

In Bulawayo, Zimbabwe, an

Christine (Herr) Pearson

exciting development began to emerge in 2005. Peter and Di Cunningham set aside for Horizon 180 acres of land on their ostrich and chicken farm for the purpose of building a large Children's Village for AIDS orphans. This property was nearly taken forcibly from the Cunninghams in 2002 by armed youth militia as part of the government initiative to remove white farmers from the land. In this case, however, local residents had intervened. They had been treated justly and generously by the Cunninghams and had stepped forward and protested to the militia, insisting: "For years you have ruled us and haven't taken care of us; but these people are righteous and have cared for us. You will have to kill us before you take their land from them!" The land was not taken.

Peter Cunningham

The land is strategically situated near a public school and Baptist congregation. Horizon orphans, once identified, sponsored, and located here, would be able to learn a range of life skills and trades – ostrich and chicken farming, agriculture, carpentry, welding, etc. This property offered an ideal location for the care of hundreds of orphans in the villages outside the city of Bulawayo. Accomplishment of this goal has been slow because of lack of funding, but the vision and potential remain great.

A vision and a plan emerged in 2008 related to an important new ministry development in the area of Fort Portal in southwestern Uganda. Situated in the foothills of the Rwenzori Mountains, this area is where Horizon already was sponsoring over 200 orphans, with many more anxiously waiting for help. The new ministry possibility for Horizon involved building a vocational school that would help older orphans learn a trade and thus prepare themselves for productive employment after their sponsorships ended. Horizon's local partner organization, *Horizon Uganda*, had been given about fifty prime acres of land by a local church member. Learning of this, Dan Smith, an American businessman, offered to donate some portable buildings for placing on the land. God appeared to be putting together all that was needed to begin. The future of this and other projects, although somewhat unclear at times, is always full of hope!

RETREATING FORWARD

The multi-nation expansion of Horizon International has greatly increased the need for networking and resourcing Horizon's growing but geographically separated staff in southern and eastern Africa. A need was soon sensed that had not existed before. Horizon had found itself actively ministering in multiple sites in South Africa, Zimbabwe, Zambia, and Uganda – and about to enter Kenya. The several regional coordinators and project directors of Horizon in Africa had Horizon's president, Robert Pearson, as their only common link. This was how it had to be at first, but a new time and a new set of circumstances were emerging for Horizon. Soon Doug Ehrgott would join Horizon's full-time staff in the United States and begin leading groups of Americans to Africa, becoming for them a second face of Horizon. Meantime, another means of team-building had arisen and gained major significance on the African side of the Atlantic Ocean.

Horizon's regional coordinators and project directors were requesting the opportunity to meet face-to-face to build acquaintance, inspire and resource each other, and do strategic planning for Horizon's present and future ministries. Organizational solidarity and common vision were extremely important. These many African ministry partners wanted to begin seeing the bigger picture and know each other as members of one Horizon *team*. The cost to do this would be considerable, but the need was real and hardly optional. Praying, planning, and fundraising began. The result was the first All-Africa Team Retreat. Cassie and Jenny Carstens volunteered to host the gathering in Capetown, South Africa. The days together would be August 18-21, 2005. They provided a time of backing away from constant routines to allow reflection and projection, and to do it *together*.

In the process of this first retreat experience, each person shared family history, ministry calling, and the progress in ministry efforts with

Doug Ehrgott entertaining children

Doug Ehrgott

Horizon to date. The group looked for ways to help each other. One practical way soon identified involved a cooperative means of getting needed food to the some 130 orphans currently being sponsored through Horizon in Harare, Zimbabwe. Serious trouble was brewing in that country, an important one for Horizon. The increasingly hostile environment already had caused World Vision, Campus Crusade for Christ, and many other non-government ministry organizations to leave the country. It would be different for Horizon, despite the trouble and danger.

Government corruption and mismanagement and dramatically rising inflation rates were making it difficult for the Horizon team in Harare to secure adequate supplies of quality food for the children on a consistent basis. Tatenda and Lucia Gunguwo of Harare had shared this problem at the retreat. The regional coordinators of Limpopo Province in South Africa had an idea. Andries and Nelly van der Merwe would purchase food and truck it to the Zimbabwean border. It could be picked up by the Gunguwos and taken to Harare. The first food transfer actually happened in October, 2005, with the van der Merwes actually taking it all the way to Harare. No one could see at the time that in 2008 there would be a dangerous political crisis in Zimbabwe that would require such food transfers from South Africa as a matter of survival for many of Horizon's children (see detail in chapter six).

The second African Team Retreat convened at the Magnab Safari Lodge in Limpopo Province, South Africa, from July 19 to 23, 2006. Twenty-five Horizon team partners from South Africa, Uganda, and Zimbabwe heard ministry reports from each other, began a strategic planning process, identified areas of need, and refined the child sponsorship program guidelines. The retreat cost was $18,000, "some of the best money we can ever spend" according to president Pearson. At the first retreat, this multi-nation Horizon team had become *friends*. At this 2006 retreat, they became working partners, even *family* to each other.

Magnab Safari Lodge

The third African Team Retreat convened in October, 2008, in Lusaka, Zambia. The retreat theme was "Moving Toward a Preferable Future," with the Sunday worship and daily devotions led by Rev. Dr. Moses Rumano, native of Zimbabwe, a United Methodist minister. and likely a future leader of Horizon in Africa. This amazing "team" of African leaders was now truly a family, a coordinated force for good serving in God's name in southern and eastern Africa. This 2008 gathering of Horizon's African leaders sensed the hand of God on their ministries. They worshipped, rejoiced, and worked together, helped in part by the administrative skill of Gayla Morgan from the home offices in the United States.

Convinced that it was only the beginning of their ministries together, the Lusaka, Zambia, retreat group clarified strategies, intensified relationships, and honed administrative skills so that they could function more effectively in their respective places of ministry. They also played together. Chadd Bain from South Africa was the ring leader in organizing a soccer game between a local orphan group and a group of the "old ones" at the retreat. No one had any idea what would happen a year later. The African team circle would be broken by tragedy.

It happened in December of 2009. Chadd Bain was killed in a road accident back in South Africa. Horizon leaders in the United States and in Africa were shocked and rallied to be supportive in every way possible of Chadd's wife Kate and their

The 2008 African Team Retreat

children. As only one example of support, this book of Horizon's history is dedicated to Chadd Bain, special servant of God. Grief, something so well known in Africa, would have to be endured and somehow made into an open door to an unknown but productive tomorrow.

THINKING AHEAD WITH GOD

Mundane matters at Horizon's home offices in Pendleton, Indiana, continue to demand attention. Handling them well helps to keep ministry on the other side of the Atlantic Ocean from faltering. Trying to upgrade furniture and equipment is a constant challenge. The ministry's offices have always been housed in limited and rented facilities. By late 2007 the cramped quarters across from the local high school were becoming unworkable. Fortunately, the owner was able to make available an adjacent part of the building, very welcome new space. During 2008, however, president Pearson was informed that the owner, generous as he is, could guarantee only two more years of Horizon occupancy. This uncertainty and growing space needs made it prudent to lay some plans for a facility of Horizon's own. Fulfilling this need would require substantial funds not in hand. Thus, adequate facilities remains a major challenge not yet addressed.

The Horizon staff in the home offices has continued to grow and provide invaluable service, despite the many limitations. At the close of 2009, a skilled and dedicated group of staff women were laboring daily in Pendleton, Indiana. What would be mundane, even maddening for some, was truly ministry for them. As they sought to handle the many details generated by the greatly enlarged ministry, even more was in the planning stage for 2010 and beyond. Office staff in the home offices of Horizon would labor faithfully with the endless details of administration and numerous Americans would continue to pray, give, and sometimes go to Africa personally – some like Morris and Jo Walter multiple times.

The May, 2007, meeting of Horizon's board of directors discussed at length the issue of an appropriate strategy for facing further expansion of its African ministries. Horizon was then actively at work in multiple locations in South Africa, Zimbabwe, Uganda, and Zambia, with new

The staff in Horizon's home offices

possibilities on the table in these countries. In addition, expansion requests had been received from the Democratic Republic of the Congo, Ethiopia, and Mozambique. Partner organizations of Horizon stretched widely and could easily spread Horizon's ministry. Among others, they included *Kuyasa Horizon Empowerment, Horizon Thusanang, Voice of Peace, Horizon Uganda,* the *African Leadership Institute for Community Transformation, Heart of Africa,* and the *International Sports Coalition.* The related questions were numerous and were addressed by the board, at least in a preliminary way.

What was the voice of God saying? Where was the need and opportunity the greatest? Was adequate funding available for new ministries? How could quality new ministry partners be recruited? What would more expansion do to existing ministries? It was reported to the board of directors that the AIDS pandemic likely would expand dramatically in India and China in the years ahead. Should this fact guide expansion decisions? There were known potential donors and existing relationship networks already in India – should this guide Horizon that way? The board affirmed a world vision of ministry and was not prepared to close any doors. However, it was determined not to become an organization that overextends itself, finally functioning "a mile wide and an inch deep." Integrity of any new ministry launches was judged crucial. It was not yet clear that expanding to more countries was appropriate, especially beyond Horizon's original mission focus on southern and eastern Africa.

Jo and Morris Walter

A significant danger to Horizon's very viability was recognized and addressed by the board of directors. In its earliest years, Horizon's entire ministry was based on the vision and network of people built and nurtured by Robert Pearson, founder and current president. He was the one prominent face of Horizon in Africa and the United States. While the most recent years have seen the organization grow much "bigger than Bob," the danger remained. What if something happened to the president, something like happened suddenly to Chadd Bain? After all, Pearson often travels long distances for Horizon, including in some dangerous places in Africa. Thus, the importance of a plan for presidential succession had become obvious. In its meeting of May 19, 2007, the board of directors of Horizon formally considered this issue and reviewed a preliminary plan for presidential succession should an emergency of this kind ever arise.

And what about the periodic crises that burst forth from unexpected sources and threaten the already existing ministries? Hope may always be on the horizon, but it also is true that hope always seems to have its enemies. That tragic day that took the life of Chadd Bain was one such enemy. One of a different kind had flared on November 3, 2008. It stands as a fitting symbol of what can happen at any time – and what God can do despite whatever happens.

A Horizon ministry team from Highland Park Community Church

in Casper, Wyoming, had been working at the Matipane Orphan Drop-in Center in Limpopo Province, South Africa. While these dedicated Americans were at work, a fire started in the hills overlooking the Magnab Safari Lodge, the temporary and very gracious home for many Horizon mission groups over the years. With the work team back at the Lodge near evening, the wind shifted and the huge fire began coming right at them, with smoke filling the grounds and hot embers drifting down to the rooftops from the red sky! They quickly packed and fled to a tomato farm three kilometers away.

Horizon's president, Robert Pearson, was there and began praying that God would spare Magnab for the sake of the orphaned children of the region. He also asked to be taken back to the Lodge so that he could help the frantic owners, Boetlap and Dalene Pohl, finish evacuating. Then it happened. After a long dry spell that had made this fire possible, the sky suddenly darkened and then opened with a downpour of rain. By the time Pearson reached the Lodge, the fire was almost a thing of the past!

A dramatic event like this is open to more than one interpretation. Boetlap Pohl was convinced that it had been an act of God. He had grown up on this property. In four decades, he had never seen rain approach from all four directions simultaneously. This time it did, and it had dumped its healing water directly on the fire – and it had rained only until the fire was out!

What was left of the property, and what could be learned from this frightening event? It wouldn't take long to find out. A week later, Robert Pearson and Boetlap Pohl traveled for two hours in a four-wheeler to access the damage to the area. Their eyes were filled with a surprising goodness, a gift of God. Hope was clearly on this horizon. The fire had enriched the soil – grass was already breaking through and in a month the whole area would be carpeted with new grass and colorful flowers. The previous jungle of dry undergrowth that would have had to be cleared for the sake of the wildlife, and at a cost of millions of South African Rand, was gone! The fire had done the job well, and for nothing. God sometimes works in mysterious ways, but God's work will get done, somehow, sometime. Hope remains on the horizon of all the fires of our lives and ministries.

An African parable presents well the mission and continuing resolve of Horizon International as it proceeds to minister in the midst of very difficult and unpredictable circumstances. This parable roots in a real event. It happened to a group of Horizon work campers visiting Krueger

National Park, a large game reserve in Limpopo Province, South Africa. The group, riding in a car, noticed two adult elephants, with another one close by that was very young. The three of them were standing close to the road. Everyone naturally was anxious to stop and take pictures. One of the adult elephants, however, began to stamp the ground, ears up and dirt being thrown by its trunk. The position of the vehicle was greatly upsetting the massive animal for some reason.

Then it happened. Another adult elephant, previously unnoticed, stood on the opposite side of the road, also accompanied by a young one. The agitated elephant began charging toward the car! Only a tree in its path slowed it down, giving the vehicle a chance to escape disaster. Why had this happened? The alien humans had accidentally strayed into the middle of a herd of elephants that were being separated from each other by the vehicle, and the charging elephant obviously felt that the babies were in danger. It would act as necessary to protect the young.

Now comes the parable growing from this incident. And what about

Michelle Canada with future leaders of Zimbabwe, orphans with hope because of the generosity of people like you, the reader

Horizon International? It has been designed to be such an agitated elephant. HIV/AIDS has forced its horrible self into the midst of the human scene, separating families and disrupting whole societies. The young of the world are paying the greatest price. Since 2001, and into the foreseeable future, Horizon International has acted dramatically, and will continue to do all that it can to save the innocent and orphaned children. It will put itself at risk in order to rejoin families and heal the tragic results of an alien invasion.

Horizon's current attitude and future intent are conveyed well in the words of a member of its board of directors and Horizon's vice-president, Christopher Dancy:

I find no fatigue in this work, but instead energy and excitement. I am finding more and more areas of need where I can serve and make a difference. What a marvelous path God has put me on!

The president of Horizon, Robert Pearson, also intends to continue his tireless ministry on behalf of African orphans. Recalling that initial dream that fired the future for him (see chapter one), he now has made clear that he is not looking to be a martyr. Even so, he would rather lose his life in the service of Jesus than bask in the comfort of the sidelines, ignoring what is happening in the world. God is thinking ahead, always ahead. So, with the help and vision of God, there can be no fatigue allowed to delay this work, only energy and excitement!

In a 2005 sermon, Pearson recalled Ruby Dodzo, then an orphan living in a *Voice of Peace* home in Harare, Zimbabwe. He had asked her about her dreams for the future. She had looked at him as if to say, "Who in my country can afford to dream?" Pearson had said to her, "Now that your survival needs are met and you know Jesus, it's time for you to *start dreaming*!" Hundreds, no, now thousands of Africa's young have heard Horizon leaders say that very thing to them over and over. This is what they have heard: "The future waits, God calls and gifts, and your troubled nations need new leaders at every level. Why not you?"

A big and very personal dream of Robert Pearson himself finally was realized. He found a life companion who now is bringing great new joy to both his own life and that of Horizon International. On September 12, 2009, he married Christine Herr, an Indiana nurse with a great heart for people, a deep Christian commitment, and a growing passion for

Horizon's work in Africa. This was a blessing long awaited and widely celebrated. The wedding ceremony featured Horizon board members and spouses creating a canopy with flags of the African nations being served by Horizon. Robert and Christine were inspired by and committed to each other and the desperate children of these nations whose colors were being paraded proudly. After the wedding, the Pearsons traveled together to Horizon ministry sites in Africa, enjoying locally arranged receptions celebrating their marriage and looking with excitement to the future.

Christine and Robert Pearson in their African wedding attire

One day, by God's grace, and partly through Horizon's ministries, orphaned children by the thousands will have been enabled to survive their desperate circumstances. Having escaped the HIV/AIDS pandemic and early death, they will have rediscovered the reality of "family." They will be well in body and whole in spirit, rejoicing in Jesus Christ and rebuilding their African societies with a vision of a better future. They will constitute a new generation of healthy, educated, and deeply-committed Christian Africans. The prayer of Horizon is, *"Dear God, may it be so!"*

APPENDIX A
History of Horizon Leadership: United States and Africa

	2001	2002	2003	2004
CORPORATE OFFICERS:				
President	RP	RP	RP	RP
Vice President	ED	ED	ED	ED
Secretary	BC	BC	BC	BC
Treasurer	JJ	JJ	JJ	JJ
BOARD OF DIRECTORS:				
Members	RP, ED, BC, JJ BP, MJ	RP, ED, BC, JJ	RP, ED, BC, JJ	RP, ED, BC, JJ
U. S. OFFICE STAFF:				
Operations				
Child Sponsorship Coor.			JC	JC
Communications Coor.				
Global Team Builders				
Office Manager				
Administrative Asst.				
Accounts: Receivable/Payable				
Gift Shop Sales Staff				DW
FIELD REPRESENTATIVES:				
United States		JJO	JJO, D/RM	JJO, DRM
AFRICAN REGIONAL COORDINATORS:				
South Africa		J/CC	J/CC, A/NV	J/CC, A/NV
Kenya				
Uganda				
Zambia				
Zimbabwe		T/LG	T/LG	T/LG

2005	2006	2007	2008	2009	2010
RP	RP	RP	RP	RP	RP
ED	ED	ED	ED	ED	CD
BC	BC	BC	BC	BC	BC
(BC)	(BC)	BP	BP	BP	BP
RP, ED, BC, CD, BP, MJ	RP, ED, BC, CD, BP, MJ, LS	RP, ED, BC, CD, BP, MJ, LS	RP, ED, BC, CD, BP, LS	RP, ED, BC, CD, BP, LS	RP, ED, BC, CD, BP, LS
MC	MC				
JC	JC	GM	GM	GM	GM
	CL	AS	--	--	--
				D/SE	D/SE
		SF	SF	SF	SF
SF	SF		MR	LM	LM
		CF, AW	CF, BB	BB, RD, SL	BB, RD, SL
DW	DW	DW	DW	DW	DW
JJO, D/RM	JJO, D/RM	DC, D/RM	D/RM, W/NC, T/JD	D/RM, W/NC, T/JD	D/RM, W/NC, T/JD, T/CK
J/CC, A/NV	J/CC, A/NV	J/CC, A/NV	J/CC, A/NV	J/CC, A/NV	J/CC, A/NV
					G/RL
S/BA	S/BA	S/BA	S/BA	S/BA	S/BA
		AJ	AJ		
T/LG, A/VP	T/LG, A/VP	T/LG, A/VP	T/LG, A/VP	T/LG, A/VP	T/LG, A/VP

Brittany Kier Bayliss

Shirley Leonard

Jerry Jones

Diane Wilkinson

The Horizon
ministry is
dependent on
the efforts
of many
skilled staff
and volunteers

Randee Doe

Amanda Scott

Daniel and Ruth Murrell

Appendix A: Legend

For the Horizon leadership roles and years
as identified on pages 242-243

AJ – Ansie Joubert

A/NV – Andries and
     Nelly van der Merwe

AS – Amanda Scott

A/VP – Alick and Vidah Phiri

AW – Alicia Witkop

BB – Brittany Kier Bayliss

BC – Barry Callen

BP – Bonnie Powlison

CD – Christopher Dancy

CF – Cindy Faulkner

CL – Cassie Lomison

D/RM – Daniel and
     Ruth Murrell

D/SE – Doug and Sandy Ehrgott

DW – Diane Wilkinson

ED – Eric Dwiggins

GM – Gayla Morgan

G/RL – Gladys and
     Robert Lang'at

JC – Joyce Chapple

J/CC – Jenny and Cassie Carstens

JJ – Jeffery Jenness

JJO – Jerry Jones

LC – Lisa Scaling

LM – Lynda Malysa

MC – Michael Carey

M/CS – Moses and Cecilia Sakala

MJ – Mary Beth Jackson

MR – Mary Rickart

RD – Randee Doe

RP – Robert Pearson

S/BA – Silas and Betty Atugonza

SF – Samantha Frazier

SL – Shirley Leonard

T/CK – Timothy and
     Cynthia Kumfer

T/JD – Teresa and Jay Davidson

T/LG – Tatenda and
     Lucia Gunguwo

W/NC – Winston and
     Nancy Clark

Index
Names, Subjects, Pages, Locations